Routledge Revivals

I0121778

Sex and Citizenship

First published in 1941, *Sex and Citizenship* encourages people to think constructively about our moral problems. The author argues that sexual relationships have in the past been largely based upon self-interest. We have yet to try a moral code based upon trust, equality, and love, backed by knowledge and reason.

The book discusses themes such as moral problem; religion and science; friendship; principles of sex relationships; marriage, parents and children; marriage preparation; and the future. The philosophy and theology of this book are those of a practicing doctor who is in daily contact with these problems. This book is not intended as a theological treatise and is an important historical reference for scholars of sociology.

To

THE RIGHT HON. THE LORD HORDER
G.C.V.O., M.D., F.R.C.P.

with grateful thanks
for his unfailing encouragement
and
with sincere admiration for his
outstanding work towards human
betterment

FOREWORD

THE FOREWORDS WHICH well-meaning friends write at the request of authors differ very widely. Some are mere "puffs," written one fancies on a rather slender knowledge of the contents. Others amount almost to a critical review. Neither of these methods is very satisfactory, though the latter is at least the more honest of the two.

I have read Dr. Griffith's book with care, and I desire very definitely to commend it for careful study by all those who are concerned to understand and deal with one of the most pressing moral issues of our civilization. Unless I am mistaken, there are signs of a tendency within the last year or two to dismiss books about sex-morality with a certain impatience: there have been so many of them: the subject is becoming an obsession: with the whole structure of our civilization cracking around us, surely there are more important matters to attend to than whether men and women behave themselves in what is, after all, a private department of their lives. The great value of this book is that, as its title indicates, it puts the question of sex-morality where it belongs, in the very centre of our concern about the "new order" of human life which we are all asserting must be found.

It raises issues of the kind which are usually called "controversial". That means that it makes a serious attempt to examine certain aspects of our existing moral practice which are commonly described as "immoral", to ask whether they all equally deserve that condemnation, and to propound means of dealing with them which, in some cases, involve a re-consideration of our traditional views. Those who know Dr. Griffith's earlier volumes, and are acquainted with his work as a consulting physician, and as a lecturer in universities and public schools, will not need to be assured that the suggestions which he makes are the result of wide experience, and the expression of a most genuine desire to promote what he believes to be a healthier and a more Christian theory and practice in this sphere of human relations.

There are views expressed in the book which I myself cannot fully accept. It does not seem to me, for instance, that Dr. Griffith has devoted sufficient attention to the value which Christianity attaches to "chastity" as distinct from "celibacy" or "virginity". Nor does he appear really to face the question whether the Christian demand for pre-marital continence is not primarily based upon the conviction that an acknowledged and ratified acceptance of the responsibility of marriage and children is an absolute condition of the exercise of the "pleasure principle".

There are other questions which one could raise: but, as I said, this is a foreword, not a review. The book as a whole commends itself to me as an honest, temperate, wholesome piece of work, which has the great merit of showing the relation of the specific question of sex-morality to many other urgent issues which affect the health and well-being of the community. Not the least valuable point is the writer's insistence on the need for reforms in certain aspects of the work of his own profession.

F. A. COCKIN.

1, Amen Court,
March, 1941

PREFACE

THE PURPOSE OF this book is to encourage people to think constructively about our moral problems. There are forces abroad challenging any positive standards of behaviour, denying the value of discipline and responsibility in sex relationships, and concentrating on the pursuit of pleasure. Life moves fast and we shall be missing valuable time if we do not turn our thoughts, even now in the midst of chaotic warfare, to the creative tasks which lie ahead of us.

The ideals and hopes of many are necessarily shattered by war. We cannot be surprised, therefore, if young people do not look far ahead when making decisions that affect their personal relationships; war encourages people to think only of the present. Nevertheless, personal behaviour is no longer our own affair; it is also the concern of society. Our present moral standards, based upon religious and social influences which no longer maintain an effective brake, have largely disappeared. Thus we find ourselves without any clear principles upon which to base our sex lives. We need not necessarily be alarmed at this situation, indeed, it was to be expected because neither the social nor religious restrictions had very sound foundations. Ignorance, superstition and fear are not the right ingredients for a stable moral standard. Nevertheless, we must have a moral code; society cannot get along without one. From whence are the principles of this code to be derived? For what ideal are we striving?

If the old code is worn out the new one must be strengthened by a synthesis of scientific knowledge and religious principles. We may deny both but if we do we shall lead a life well below that which is possible; one lacking in character, stability and strength. The first essential, therefore, is to recognise that a perfect sex relationship is the outcome of a personal relationship which, by its very nature, is life long, mutually beneficial and directed towards the establishment of the family unit. Here we have an ideal which is in accord with Christian teaching and modern scientific knowledge. The establishment of principles upon which this ideal can function is not so easy. It may be argued that we do not possess sufficient scientific knowledge or spiritual understanding to find the principles. It is true that we may not discover them all, but we can certainly find some, to which we can add in the light of further knowledge and understanding. We must be willing, however, to accept new knowledge. If the essential unit of society is the family, the principles must be designed to maintain and strengthen this institution. If the family unit is not being maintained, the rest of the ideal will naturally fall to pieces. This is precisely what is happening at present. The family unit is not being maintained.

Thus we find a widespread denial of family responsibility, late marriage and fewer children. Running side by side with this state of affairs is a greatly increased knowledge of certain aspects of sex—particularly the biological, leading to a new, and by no means entirely satisfactory, outlook regarding sex behaviour, together with an increase in types of relationships which have the sanction of neither Church nor State. Whilst believing that much of this new knowledge possesses fundamental creative aspects, it is necessary to enquire if these new relationships are tending to strengthen or weaken the family unit; benefit the individuals concerned or prove of value to society. If the motive force behind them is good, we must ask ourselves what changes are necessary in our social order to make them more effective. It is obvious that we are going through a period of vast social upheaval. We must see to it that the new morality is built up on sound principles. But the principles cannot act because society will not create a suitable environment in which they can act. And so the ideal remains a long distant hope. Nevertheless, it is an ideal and if we accept it we must work towards it.

I am forced to the conclusion that we cannot expect any radical change in moral behaviour until we establish an educational background which will provide the necessary ethical and scientific training to enable young people to accept their responsibilities with some chance of success. This book, therefore, will attempt to show some of the Christian and scientific data from which our principles must be drawn; to outline the principles themselves and to consider some of the problems of sex behaviour which are of practical importance to-day. Here, in particular, it will be found that the solutions and suggestions are very often make-shift and far removed from the ideal. Nevertheless, I have attempted to provide constructive help because it is essential to be practical as well as theoretical. Wherever possible, deviations from the ideal are indicated and tentative suggestions made for their improvement. In addition, I have examined some of the environmental factors which are preventing early planned marriages and the production of wanted and desirable children. Until we achieve this end we must expect a continuation of the unsatisfactory behaviour that is so prevalent to-day. Indiscriminate sex relationships, pre-marital and extra-marital relationships, abortion, venereal disease and a whole host of psychological upsets will tend to be on the upgrade.

Sexual relationships have in the past been largely based upon self-interest. We have yet to try a moral code based upon trust, equality and love, backed by knowledge and reason. We have a great opportunity if only we will take it. It would be possible, with courage, determination and organization, for the bodies concerned with these matters to get together and formulate a positive scheme of moral reconstruction that would appeal to young people throughout the country.

The philosophy and theology of this book are those of a practising doctor who is in daily contact with these problems. The book is not intended as a theological treatise even if the writer were capable of producing one. There is nothing here that I do not believe needs saying, indeed, I think that most people with any knowledge of these problems will agree that I have not overstated the position.

The correctness of some of my statements cannot be judged on personal experience alone. Many people are leading very happy sex lives, and have never come across the problems I am discussing. That does not mean that they do not exist, nor that the sex lives of many so-called "happily married" couples would not have been even happier and more harmoniously adjusted had they at the beginning of their own marriages received some of the information we can now impart.

If some who read this book are constrained to pause and reflect that by their hasty or ill-thought-out behaviour they may be hazarding two of the most valuable things in life—their own and another's personality—I shall feel rewarded.

It is impossible to acknowledge sufficiently the debt I owe to numerous friends, who by their conversation and willingness to read and criticise the manuscript have been of immense help in stimulating and clarifying my own thought.

February, 1941.

Harley Street, W.1.

CONTENTS

Foreword   *Page* 7

Preface   9

Chapter I.   The Moral Problem   15

      II.   Religion and Science   31

      III. Growing Up   43

      IV.   Friendship   60

      V.   Principles of Sex Relationships   72

      VI.   Sex Relationships and Society   86

      VII. Marriage, Parents and Children   114

      VIII. Sexual Maladjustments   136

      IX.   Betrothal and Marriage Preparation   153

      X.   The Future   160

            Appendix A. "Material for Lecture
            Courses" prepared by the Marriage
            Guidance Council   205

            Appendix B. "To Those About to
            Marry." Pamphlet issued by the British
            Social Hygiene Council   211

Bc

THE MORAL PROBLEM

I find the great thing in this world is not so much where you
stand, as in what direction we are moving; to reach the port
of heaven, we must sail sometimes with the wind, and sometimes against it—but we must sail, and not drift, nor lie at
anchor.

OLIVER WENDELL HOLMES. 1809-1894

MAN IS A social animal to whom friendship and
companionship are essential. His life is necessarily affected
by his reactions to others and his behaviour is regulated
by a series of social laws designed to make him a useful
member of society. If his personality is properly attuned
to the society in which he lives, he will become useful;
if it is not, he will develop anti-social traits which will
bring him into conflict with his fellow beings. Personal
relationships, therefore, are primarily concerned with
conduct, and are largely regulated by the customs and
laws of the country in which we live. This book, which is
primarily concerned with the personal relationships of
men and women, will necessarily pay considerable attention to the aspect of sex.

Not only have we discovered much within recent years
about the nature and meaning of sex, but modern conditions have profoundly changed our attitude towards the
whole subject. For many people marriage must be post-
poned if the individual is to make satisfactory headway
against the excessive competition of every-day life. This
in itself is a serious matter and creates a multitude of
difficulties. In addition, there is a general speeding up,
an increase in nervous tension and an excessive emphasis

on emotional life, to complicate the problem of right conduct.

Sex is still to many people an evil burden whose nature they find shameful or sinful, mainly because they are unable to understand its true meaning. Most of the rules of conduct create in our minds a powerful guilt sense. By considering the scientific data now available, we will try to formulate principles which will enable us to take a more positive view of the problems of personal relationships. In addition, because sex is, and always has been, intimately concerned with religious feeling, we will attempt to find a working relationship between these two, which are often unfortunately considered mutually antagonistic.

SOME FUNDAMENTAL PRINCIPLES

Several fundamental principles form the essential background of our discussion.

We must recognise that, as civilisation is at present constituted, the family is the basis of society. Any loosening of the moral code which tends to destroy this fundamental unit is obviously anti-social. There is evidence enough of this and a further discussion of the matter is outside the scope of this book.[1]

Secondly, we shall take it as agreed that monogamy is the natural order of an enlightened society. Havelock Ellis states that "monogamic marriage is a natural biological fact alike in many animals and in men."[2] Monogamy, indeed, may have developed from an earlier state of polygamy, but the arguments in favour of the institution of polygamy are usually advanced by men and based on self-interest. Professor Westermarck considers the evidence in considerable detail and concludes that little would be gained by legalised polygamy (multiple wives). "Any proposal to that effect would undoubtedly be rejected, not

---

[1] See, for instance, *Three Essays on Sex and Marriage*, by Dr. Westermarck.

[2] *Sex in Relation to Society*, p. 338

only as being generally unwanted by the men, but also as being degrading to the women and contrary, to public feeling."[1]

We must presume, therefore, that in any future re-organisation of society, monogamy will form the basis of the social code, although the law may be modified in certain respects.

The reader will be asked to accept thirdly that the sexes are complementary to each other; that whilst biologically different they only reach a perfect development through mutual companionship, involving mind, spirit, and body. Men and women are essentially equal, though there are wide differences in function and construction. Each has his or her contribution to make to the development of the personality of the other, and neither should dominate the other. Only by recognising these principles will the individual character be developed to its fullest capacity. Its acceptance demands a considerable change of outlook. No longer can men look upon women as playthings for their leisure hours. No longer should women be passive acceptors of physical attentions. Equality demands co-operation between free personalities, both in work and play. The differences that exist on the physical and emotional planes must be understood and respected. Neither individual should exercise his or her powers in such a way as to destroy the personality of the other. This means that each sex must develop a sense of responsibility towards the other. Men in particular must learn to work with women in an equal partnership, at school, college and in later life. This principle is fundamental to our purpose. Refusal to acknowledge it will make this book meaningless.

The effect of this co-operation on our sex relationships is discussed at length in a report of the Christian Churches issued in 1924.[2] This C.O.P.E.C. report considers that the

[1] *The Future of Marriage in Western Civilisation*, p. 193.
[2] *The Relation of the Sexes*, Vol. IV, issued by the Conference on Christian, Political and Economic Relations to Citizenship, held at Birmingham.

result will be entirely beneficial because it will develop a fellowship between the sexes in which the non-sexual interests in life take a normal place. It will broaden the relationships between husbands and wives by stimulating their interests through contact with other people. "It will greatly lessen the strain of conscious desire for unmarried men and women."[1] It will also enable young people to get to know each other in a far more satisfactory manner than has been possible. But the greater freedom must be accompanied by sound instruction.

Finally, man possesses a spiritual nature in addition to his physical and psychological make-up. Religion, however primitive its form, has existed in all civilisations; it seems to be necessary for men. We, in this country, are concerned mainly with Christianity which, by its very nature, possesses the basis for a constructive sex ethic. The past teaching of the Church with regard to sex has not been ideal. Much of to-day's scientific knowledge of sexual behaviour was a closed book to the leaders of early Christian thought. It is easy to criticise a negativism based on lack of essential knowledge but, on the other hand, it is mainly Christian insistence on the sanctity of marriage and the value of woman's personality that made our present conception of womanhood possible. No other religion or system of philosophy has demanded so high a standard of behaviour towards women. In spite of restrictions and taboos the Church has consistently fought for the maintenance of this standard. That this is equally true of the present is shown by three extracts from recent ecclesiastical pronouncements.

The C.O.P.E.C. report says: "We regard sex as a divine endowment of the human race, to be used, not to be feared. The satisfaction that it yields may be amongst the highest that can be experienced by human beings, involving not only physical and emotional delight, but the further

[1] *The Relation of the Sexes*, Vol. IV, issued by the Conference on Christian, Political and Economic Relations to Citizenship, held at Birmingham. p. 20.

bliss (we use the word advisedly) of the mutual self-surrender of the married lovers, and the self-satisfying and self-realising joys of parenthood. In this way sex ministers to the highest moral and religious development of mankind."[1]

According to the Report of the 1930 Lambeth Conference[2]: "Sex is a God-given factor in the life of mankind, and its functions are therefore essentially noble and creative. Correspondingly great is the responsibility for the right use of it."

The third extract comes from the Report of the Commission on Christian Doctrine in the Church of England issued in 1938. "The belief that the process of human generation is in itself sinful, or that sin is conveyed to the offspring because of any sinfulness in the process, is *not* a necessary part of the doctrine of original sin, and we are agreed in repudiating it. We believe that it is wholly unwarranted, being part of a profoundly unsatisfactory view of sex and of sexual relations."[3]

These are positive contributions to the sex problem which also receive support from modern psychology.

Without considering the different ethical systems in detail we can at least ask whether we are satisfied with some of the definitions of moral behaviour that exist to-day. For instance, is our main purpose in life the pursuit of pleasure? If so, how do we define "pleasure"? If, as Canon Peter Green points out, it means agreeable sensation, this is not our main purpose, because many good things which we desire have nothing to do with bodily sensations. If all virtuous conduct leads to gratification of a desire, we have no criterion "by which we may distinguish between higher and lower desires, or even between what we instinctively feel to be noble and good desires, and those we equally instinctively reject as evil."[4]

[1] C.O.P.E.C. Report, Vol. IV, p. 189.
[2] p. 85.
[3] p. 63.
[4] Canon Peter Green, *The Problem of Right Conduct*, p. 67.

Further, does the gratification of a desire necessarily lead to contentment, happiness or even satisfaction? Is it not true that, particularly in the sexual sphere, the gratification of desire by no means brings the sense of happiness and peace for which we had hoped? The reason is not far to seek. We have been concerned with the self alone and sex is not an individual affair; it involves another personality. Therefore the pursuit of pleasure for personal gratification brings no permanent satisfaction.

DETERMINISM

Determinism is a conception of behaviour very prevalent to-day. This implies that everything we do or think is the result of past events and influences, whether physical or mental; that we are what we are by reason of our heredity, environment, and psychological make-up; that all our actions are predetermined, or that our control over them is very slight. Thus, if we understood ourselves perfectly, we should know what we should do in any given set of circumstances. Such an interpretation of life is hardly sufficient to satisfy us, since it both denies the possibility of free will and omits the exercise of the reasoning faculty. "Man is more than the different parts or aspects which are ingredients of him. True knowledge of man is not, in other words, the sum total of the complete and accurate accounts of all his different aspects, even if these accounts could be made exhaustive. True knowledge is or at least includes knowledge of the man as a whole. To know a man as a whole is to know him as a personality . . . which, while it integrates all the parts, and so includes them within itself, is, nevertheless, something over and above their sum. Now to know a man as a personality is to know him in a manner of which science takes no cognisance. It is to know him as an acquaintance, and it is, for deeper knowledge, to love him as a friend."[1]

It seems then that there is some other factor which

[1] C. E. M. Joad, *Guide to the Philosophy of Morals and Politics*, p. 256.

cannot be fitted into the deterministic scheme and, as Mr. Joad also says, "it is in virtue of this factor that he is free". Thus he is enabled to make decisions, to make creative acts of will, to choose a certain line of conduct; he possesses free will. This agrees with Adler's conception of a "creative power", essential for the development of personality and the formation of character.

To act from impulse is to express a particular "part" or "bit" of oneself. "It is only in so far as man acts as a whole—as a whole, that is to say, which is more than the sum of its parts—that he may be able to escape *complete* determination by the thousand and one influences of heredity, constitution, training and so forth, that play upon him. What is popularly known as the foundation of character may then be regarded as the building up of a personality which, in so far as it is entitled to be regarded as a whole, both integrates and transcends the parts which have gone to its making."[1]

FREE WILL

If we are free we have the power of choice; we are not bound to adhere to the highest moral principles, but the strength of our character will ultimately depend upon our ability to exercise our reasoning faculties dispassionately. It is true that we are often frustrated by heredity, training and environment, or, particularly, by what Adler terms "organ inferiority". By this he means that some of us are born with physical disabilities which may affect our whole outlook on life. Some are shortsighted, or have poor constitutions. Others are so mentally warped that they are incapable of acting in accordance with the best interests of themselves or the group to which they belong. And yet who can say that they do not contribute something, however small, to the total thought and feeling of mankind?

Is our morality to be decided for us by the State, or are we, as individuals, to demand that the State shall express

[1] C. E. M. Joad, *Guide to the Philosophy of Morals and Politics*, p. 261.

our will in accordance with our personalities? Are we primarily individuals living in groups and families, or mere cogs in a State machine which can order our goings and comings, our work and play, and also our thoughts? If we submit to State domination in all these matters we base our lives on the principle of fear. However wonderful the State organisation may be, however admirable its administration, we shall have returned to that principle of government by fear and submission to unknown powers, which is the essence of primitive life and religion. Rather, do we not believe in the freedom of the individual conscience, in the capacity of man to grow and develop in a corporate community, working harmoniously and joyfully for the benefit of his family, group or nation, in accordance with the principles of love, equality and freedom? This, surely, is the principle of democracy?

The difficulty, of course, is to decide what form of action, what thought or principle is most likely to conduce to the ultimate development of the personality. We must satisfy ourselves of the goodness and justice of our actions. It is useless to be told that they are good; we must consciously recognise the fact. This is particularly true of sexual morality. It is no use being told that it is wrong, or immoral, or sinful, or ethically unjustifiable to live with another man's wife or make an unmarried woman pregnant. We must satisfy ourselves that this is so. We have, therefore, to decide whether the principles of our existence are to be based on selfish satisfaction—on the unrestricted expression of our appetites and passions—or on the principle that every individual has a personality which must not be violated.

THE MORAL IDEAL

Are our actions to be governed entirely by a biological conception of sex? Is sex merely concerned with reproduction or personal gratification? Shall we obtain the maximum sexual pleasure by satisfying our biological feelings whenever we feel inclined, irrespective of the consequences? Has one individual no responsibility to another? Is it enough, for instance, to say that coitus is permissible provided that pregnancy does not supervene; that if we take suitable precautions to prevent this we have done no harm? Is this really so? Have we not been actuated by personal desire rather than by conscious thought for the well-being of the other? It is so easy to assure ourselves that a course of action is good for the other person, and to shut out little prickings of conscience which suggest that perhaps ultimately the result may be different from what we visualise—that the conscious awakening of sex feeling in a woman, for instance, may have far deeper repercussions than we are aware of; that the avoidance of pregnancy is by no means the sum of the situation. The ability to think and act constructively in the best interests of society is one of the ultimate purposes of our develop-ment. Over and over again in weighing a course of action we must balance the personal outlook against the broader, deeper and fuller realisation of social welfare. In any case we need an ideal on which to base our morality. What is that ideal? The personal qualities composing it are easily recognisable. Goodness, truth, integrity and trust, kindness, faithfulness and the avoidance of actions which may hurt others, all belong to it. These are not physical, emotional or mental qualities but spiritual. They belong to that part of us which is over and above the sum of our other qualities. They are related to conscience and they are related to God. They must harmonise with our other qualities and they must harmonise with God—with His Will. Our ideal, therefore, must be based upon the will of God, in so far as we are aware of that Will. If we ignore these spiritual qualities and say that they do not exist we are denying the Will of God and are certainly not living up to our full capacity. Neither are we satisfying the whole of ourselves. We do not, of course, understand all about the Will of God, but in addition to spiritual insight we are given other methods by which we may understand His purpose. One of these is science; the science of biology, physiology, and psychology. These are instruments which may be used in some measure to determine His Will.

In addition to all this we must have faith—faith in Him and faith in His purpose. Faith in a cause is essential to success and calls out the highest qualities of the personality.

In order to reach this ideal we must be willing to carry out a vast scheme of reconstruction after the war; how vast, will appear as we read this book and begin to appreciate how many and various are the subjects which will have to be taken into account. If the reconstruction is to be complete all the qualities that make up personality must find their rightful place. Religion and sex are essential to men. We can no more escape from the one than from the other. Both, in their highest manifestation, are concerned with the welfare of others. No religious expression or behaviour is worth anything if it is based on self-interest. Neither is sex expression of any value so long as it is concerned with the self. They only reach their true level and only become a real asset to the personality when they are directed towards the welfare of others.

We all have, of course, anti-social tendencies and forces such as aggressiveness and selfishness, but they are neither beneficial nor positive. Hence the value of early training in those principles which will develop an unselfish personality and renounce selfish gratification.

Human nature, therefore, can only reach full maturity if the motive and purpose of the individual is directed towards those ends which are of value to the society in which he lives. In no branch of human knowledge has greater advance been made recently than in the realm of sex. Two points seem to be outstanding. The first has already been mentioned; that sex, in its highest expression, is unselfish. The other is that there is another *important purpose* in sex besides reproduction, namely the satisfaction of both individuals, not one, but both. These are fundamental and will be frequently referred to. Former systems of moral behaviour fail to satisfy us because these two basic principles were not recognised. Indeed, our moral system has, for the most part, been built up on the principle of reproduction and male satisfaction. Women have come off very badly. Modern knowledge and modern discoveries make it possible for women's needs, not only to be acknowledged, but met. To many people these two ideas will appear strange. But they must be accepted before we can hope to create a better social morality; they must be incorporated into the moral theology of the Church.

Our ideal, therefore, can be restated thus. Not only is the sex relationship life long and mutually beneficial but our social morality must be directed towards the welfare of society. It must be based upon the equality of the sexes and include the full use and understanding of all our mental, physical, emotional and spiritual powers in accordance with the Will of God.

IDEALS VERSUS PRACTICE

Throughout this discussion we shall constantly come up against the ideal on the one hand and the actual conditions of life on the other. It seems only right that whilst keeping our ideal well to the fore, and striving towards its achievement, we should temper our practice with justice and mercy. Are we justified in laying down a moral law if we cannot provide a civilisation in which that law can be practised? Have we sufficient knowledge to lay down that law? It is all very well to say that the law of the Church regarding sexual conduct is definite and must be adhered to, but it is at least permissible to ask whether the law of the Church and the principles of Christ's teaching are identical. If they are not, surely we are justified in making practical adjustments following the principles of Christ's teaching as closely as our consciences can perceive, rather than continuing to submit to a system of morals based on laws which are largely antiquated, unscientific, and out of harmony with an ideal which seems more in sympathy with the mercy and justice of Christ's teaching?

Until the way is clearer we can at least refrain from condemnation and negative criticism, remembering that in no problem of conduct are Christ's words more relevant:

"He that is without sin among you, let him first cast a stone."[1]

ORIGINAL SIN

It may not be out of place to ask ourselves how the conception of original sin fits in with a modern idea of morals. Canon Peter Green states that "no system of ethics can claim to be Christian which ignores the fact that human nature is in some way corrupt".[2] A similar statement is made by the Commission on Christian Doctrine: "it is a fact of experience that man is universally prone to sin."[3] The truth of this can be satisfactorily explained along biological lines. Indeed, as we have seen, the Commission speaks of "a racial inheritance of evil, a biological transmission of moral taint".[4] This can surely be accepted by everyone. Spiritual evils are perpetuated by the handing down of a corrupted environment and the simplest knowledge of eugenics shows that we inherit our bodily make-up, "organ inferiorities", weaknesses and strength from our parents. But if we inherit tendencies to such evil emotions as lust, avarice, and possessiveness, we equally inherit tendencies towards fellowship, self-sacrifice and affection. Environment greatly influences our behaviour and character; it is much easier to lead a useful and productive life in surroundings that are harmonious, good and beautiful.

One who is mentally or physically stunted cannot be expected to have the same broad outlook on life as one who is whole. The sins of the parents have certainly descended

[1] St. John, Chap. VIII, v. 7.
[2] *The Problem of Right Conduct*, p. 103.
[3] Report on Doctrine in the Church of England, p. 60.
[4] ibid., p. 62.

upon him. But the individual is capable of overcoming disabilities, especially physical disabilities; as witness the extraordinary capacity for psychological growth and development exhibited by many people who are physically severely handicapped. If this handicap is mental, however, the block may be so complete that development is impossible. Moral growth must likewise be limited. We are born with certain physical abilities and disabilities and with a certain degree of intelligence. If that intelligence is completely warped we are incapable of appreciating moral qualities; if it is partially deficient we too are partially limited. We can, however, learn to use the intelligence we possess; we can accept or reject moral principles, we can become selfish or unselfish, anti-social or social. A true moral standard must grow from within.

It is sometimes suggested or implied that sex thoughts are in themselves evil. But sex thoughts are a natural part of our make-up and cannot therefore be sinful. Only when we use them wrongly do we commit a sin. We use them wrongly when they are directed away from our ideal and are concerned with the self rather than the welfare of the other. Any lapse from this ideal must be regarded as sin in a greater or less degree. In this sense, we have all sinned and are all sinning because we have all failed to reach the ideal. It is a principle of moral theology that the occurrence of a thought in the mind is never a sin, but only becomes sin when approbation follows. If the thought constantly occurs it may be evidence of the cultivation of a habit which in itself is sinful.

It is sometimes suggested that those who marry are on a slightly lower spiritual plane than those who are celibate and are less likely to reach the same level of spiritual development. This is an undesirable doctrine which has crept into religious teaching and has done much to lower the dignity of marriage and the rightful appreciation of sex. Both states are equally acceptable in the sight of God and both have their own particular temptations and disadvantages.

MORAL DEVELOPMENT

We all pass through a stage of development when we are necessarily subjected to the wills and opinions of others, but, as growth proceeds, the individual must be able to determine the actual conduct of his life. "He who can only carry out the instructions of others, however obediently and skilfully, is only fitted to occupy an inferior position in the economic or social scale."[1] As development progresses the individual forms his own conception of right conduct which varies according to the level reached. He may be concerned with his own immediate benefit or he may advance to the plane on which he is concerned with the well-being of another or of humanity as a whole.

We possess a dual capacity; an urge to satisfy the desires of the self, and also an urge to live fully in contact with the community. Freud says that mental health can only be attained when what he terms the love-force is directed away from the self to other people and things. Love must be focused on others, and must concern itself with their well-being. And in order to love it is essential to be loved. This fact is very important for education. Many psychologists regard adequate love and security in infancy as the basic factor determining the child's future development. A loving environment calls forth the love of the child; parental disharmony produces the opposite effect.

We can go farther. Adler shows that it is essential for the individual to free himself from a sense of infantile inferiority, and to advance from the easy life of dependence to that of complete independence. "The individual must feel himself to be with a *meaning*, for he cannot have human importance without it."[2] We must free ourselves from a feeling of inferiority and of frustration which leads to illness. This can only be done by recognising the need to live in the community so that we may find individual

[1] Professor Flugel, *The Psycho-Analytical Study of the Family*, p. 44.
[2] Mairet, *A.B.C. of Adler's Psychology*, p. 65.

freedom and peace. In return for this willingness to serve the community society must provide adequate facilities for service. The starved individual will become selfish and greedy. This is particularly true of sex. "Love must not be given by the self to the self. . . . There must be established between the self and others a love relationship of give and take on which the lives of all depend."[1] We must advance and live, or retreat into ourselves and die. Here is the difficulty. There is always the fight between the progressive elements of our nature and the self-seeking, timid, uncreative side that is striving to remain in, or return to, the protection provided by our infantile life. Maturity is only reached by a willingness to venture into the unknown. Man is, as Jung says, to some extent master of his own destiny. To grow, man must keep in touch with the "great wisdom of life, the Christian faith".[2] Life is progressive, growing ever outwards, re-creating itself. Here, surely, we have the beginning of that process to which the term "re-birth" was applied by Christ.

It is no good considering the past or even the present. Only the future shows hope of greater creative progress —or re-birth—"of raising life's intensity to its highest pitch".[3] This desire for self-creation is within us all and forms the basis of moral behaviour.

It is impossible to achieve "re-birth" without accepting the friendship offered by the Spirit of God to vivify the creative urge of man. Such a religion demands strength, courage, and fortitude. The giving up of the self, which is the essence of modern psychological teaching, is also the central idea of Christ's teaching. One does not have to believe every article of the Creed to follow this.

Much of this energy, this life force, must be transferred to others, and to achieve this we need courage and the stimulation of friendship. Grace Stuart suggests that it is logical to assume that human friendship requires completion

---

[1] Grace Stuart, *The Achievement of Personality*, p. 102.
[2] ibid., p. 90.
[3] Jung, *Analytical Psychology*, p. 277.

through friendship with God, which is often found through friendship with others. [1]

We are collecting more and more knowledge of the conditions under which mind, spirit and body can work together in harmony. That we cannot exclude one or accentuate the other without serious effect upon the whole personality is becoming more generally acceptable. Sexual power has been wasted, distorted, mismanaged and laughed at for so long that we are almost oblivious of its positive nature. Its relation to religion is as fundamental as its relation to science. Consequently, it is blatantly unreasonable to regard sex as an evil because it is subject to misuse. A fully developed personality is impossible without sex, although every individual does not necessarily use sexual energy in a physical way. Therefore, the presence and power of sex must be consciously recognised and accepted by everyone.

We are beginning to recognise that the instinctive urge towards physical union is not all that is necessary to make the union a success. Knowledge and understanding of technique combined with an appreciation of the emotional and psychological differences and needs of the two sexes must be added to this instinctive drive. Both partners must derive that measure of emotional benefit from the relationship that will unify the act with the total personality. Reproductive consequences may follow; these are not a constant result of the sex act in normally fertile people since we have discovered scientific means by which reproduction may be regulated.

If sex is essential to a fully balanced personality it is equally true that a fully balanced personality forms the proper setting in which sex can act. A mere physical interpretation of sex is inadequate because it ignores the other essential factors that form the fully developed individual. The more we study the scientific aspects of sex—and in this matter we cannot separate physiology and biology from psychology—the more apparent it will

---

[1] Grace Stuart, *The Achievement of Personality*, p. 96

be that a purely materialistic interpretation is unsound; that sexual activity viewed as a mere physical exercise brings dissatisfaction and disillusionment. Physical satiation produces just as unstable a personality as does the refusal to accept sex as a natural part of life.

We have touched very briefly on various fundamentals that appear essential to a proper appreciation of our problem and have stated an ideal both for the individual and society. If the national conscience regarding personal and social behaviour is to develop along right lines positive scientific knowledge must be incorporated with a living religion. Apart from the psychological differences between men and women, the distinction between the sex and reproductive acts, and the advance in contraceptive knowledge, to which we have drawn attention and which will receive further consideration later on, there are other scientific factors, which must needs be considered when we are discussing the relationship between religion and science in this field.

CHAPTER II

RELIGION AND SCIENCE

For in the brain which we term the seat of reason, there is not anything of moment more than I can discover in the crany of a beast; and this is a sensible and no inconsiderable argument of the inorganity of the soul, at least in that sense we usually so receive it. Thus we are men, and we know not how; there is something in us that can be without us, and will be after us; though it is strange that it hath no history what it was before us, nor cannot tell how it entered in us.

SIR THOMAS BROWNE. 1605–1682

THAT THERE IS a strong reaction from traditional religious teaching amongst vast sections of the population is, of course, true, but a reaction from traditional religion is by no means the same thing as a reaction from God.

Some religious people are the hardest on earth and some of the most cruel persecutions the world has ever known have been made in the name of religion. Such people have lost the Love which is the essence of their faith. They have been more concerned with maintaining certain "truths" than with the development of their personality. But religious feeling is not static. It is dynamic and full of growth and energy. Is it not natural that as we grow up we discard outworn doctrines? This does not mean that we throw over principles provided we know what the principles are. That is the trouble at the present time. We are not certain of our principles. We are not certain that our present moral code expresses the true nature of God as taught by Christ. Is it not a healthy sign that we are willing to re-think our position in the light of modern knowledge, if by so doing we can arrive at a fuller conception of life? There is much evidence from the writings of various well-known scientists that they are by no means satisfied with a purely materialistic interpretation of life; that there is something above and beyond—some guiding purposive force that rules and directs the world. There is little doubt that this guiding force acts through and is approached by means of the mind. It is necessary to distinguish clearly between brain and mind. The former is the instrument of the latter. The mind expresses itself by means of the brain whose areas can be mapped out with great accuracy.

The mind has always led the body in its evolutionary struggle and it is the mind which shows purpose, direction and creative energy. According to Sir Charles Sherrington there "is something in the brain that is above and beyond the obvious mechanical side of it".[1]

We inherit the characteristics of former generations through our sex cells so that we can truly say that although the body dies, something is left and passed on to future generations. In this sense we are immortal; but does the character and personality of the individual die when

[1] Dr. Greenwood, *Biology and Christian Belief*, p. 101.

the body dies? Is it not possible that by creating mind, a method has been devised by which immortality is not lost? Is it not through the mind that our personality relates itself to the infinite—to the master mind? The body may die but the mind persists. Therein lies man's personal immortality. But there is also a collective immortality. All our minds contribute something to the sum total—to the group mind. "No individual mind can equal in power and intensity the richness of feeling included in the group mind."[1]

Psychological science does not deny immortality. It shows that the mind is a reality with its own principles of action and thus forms the scientific medium through which the Spirit of God may work. It seems, therefore, that a materialistic interpretation of life is far from being able to explain the whole of life, nor is it satisfactory to man

Speaking as a biologist, Professor Julian Huxley presents the same idea. He asks what is the most fundamental need of man and suggests that "his deepest need was to discover something, some being or power, some force or tendency, which was moulding the destinies of the world—something not himself, greater than himself, with which he yet felt that he could harmonise his nature, in which he could repose his doubts, through faith in which he could achieve confidence and hope".[2] His essays are an attempt to show "how the facts of evolutionary biology provide us, in the shape of a veritable doctrine of progress, with one of the elements most essential to any externally-grounded conception of God, to any construction which shall be able to serve as permanent satisfaction of the deepest need whereof we have spoken".[3]

The physical development of man has probably finished. Athletics and medicine and scientific breeding will not bring about radical alterations in the human type, although

[1] Dr. R. B. Cattell, *Psychology and the Religious Quest*, p. 64. Nelson.
[2] Julian Huxley, *Essays of a Biologist*, p. 17, Penguin Series.
[3] ibid., p. 19.

they may eliminate physical failures and abnormalities. In the spiritual and psychological field, however, there are immense possibilities. Indeed we have hardly ventured into this comparatively unknown realm. It seems therefore that psychology, by providing man with a fuller understanding of his mind, may enable him to tap unknown sources of strength and release him from many of his miseries.

A recognition of the spiritual possibilities in man and a refusal to accept a purely materialistic outlook is of immense importance when we consider our personal behaviour and sex relationships. If our outlook on life is purely materialistic, our fundamental conception of behaviour towards the opposite sex must differ from that which we should adopt were we to believe that our friends were personalities; that our bodily construction was God-given and amenable to the influences of a master-mind.

Science enables us to visualise life as having a creative purpose in which there is direction, responsibility and consequence; not as something fortuitous. It is vitally important that there should be a genuine understanding between science and religion so that these discoveries may be incorporated into a fuller code of moral behaviour.

It is in the psychological field that we must look for a final synthesis between science and religion. Whilst psychology does not deny religion it does oppose two things:

1. A theoretical religious dogmatism which asserts false and dubious propositions unnecessary to true religion.

2. A practical religious dogmatism, when this tries to enforce rules which have outlived their usefulness, especially in regard to the place of sex in life.

But since some people wish to identify outworn traditions with Christianity, let us consider Christ's teaching.

THE TEACHING OF CHRIST

We have already drawn a distinction between Christ's teaching and the dogmatic laws laid down by his followers.

Much of Christ's teaching is revealed by His way of life, and by the principles that He gave us rather than by what He said. Christ did not propound a new ethical law. He accepted the Jewish law as being, in the main, a right expression of God's will. He did, however, direct men's attention away from the rules which lay on the surface of the "Law" to the principles which gave rise to them. The most famous example of this is His assertion that the whole of the "Law and the Prophets" is contained in the two commandments: "Thou shalt love the Lord thy God with all thy heart, and with all thy soul, and with all thy mind. This is the first and great commandment. And the second is like unto it. Thou shalt love thy neighbour as thyself."[1]

We are here primarily concerned with the second commandment—with ethics rather than devotion—but the fulfilment of the first is for Christ the condition of the fulfilment of the second. As to love God with sincerity we must love man, so also we cannot love man perfectly unless we love God. Perhaps the most prominent principles of Christ's personal ethic are the importance of motive and the renunciation of personal rights.

Christ is in complete accord with modern psychological knowledge in stressing the importance of motive—that an act is not to be considered by itself, but as the symptom of a total attitude to life. Only when the heart of man is good can the good act arise. For instance, it is not enough to behave correctly to those we dislike; we must endeavour truly to understand them, to look for their good qualities and appreciate them. This, surely, is what is meant by the term "loving your enemies". Christ would say that it is not enough to avoid hurting a person; we must "love" him, understand him and sympathise with him. We must get under his skin, as it were, and find out what he is really like if we are to "know" him. And Christ would say that

[1] St. Matthew, Chap. XXII, v. 37-39. See also St. Luke, Chap. X, v. 25-27 for a development of the ideal relationship to one's neighbour in the parable of the Good Samaritan.

this change of heart can only come about through God's action. "We can only love our enemies if we pray or them." We can only do this through spiritual power.

This principle of unselfish love and understanding which is the spiritual root of all our actions applies to sex, the sexual act, and the sexual thought. It is on this principle that the basis of marriage rests. There must be real love, understanding and sympathy for the other person for a fully harmonious relationship to become possible. The bad traits, the little annoyances and deficiencies of the other must be overcome by the deeper and stronger power of sympathetic love and affection, which comes from a really understanding heart.

The second principle—the renunciation of personal rights—is well illustrated in the Sermon on the Mount. The individual is not to assert his "rights". I am not to defend my property at law just because it is mine nor to revenge an insult just because my vanity—my precious self—has been insulted. I am to regard my neighbour unselfishly and with toleration because I do not know him—God alone can do that. Christ gives this principle again in the parable of the unmerciful servant who is so much in debt to the kindness of his Master that his assertion of legal rights against his fellow servant becomes ridiculous. We shall see presently that the assertion of personal "rights" in the sexual relationship leads to the disruption of that relationship and is contrary to every scientific principle of sexual behaviour.

Christ had to deal with the Jewish marriage laws which gave to the man and woman unequal rights of divorce. They were unfair laws, quite contrary to the principles of equality that He taught.

Let us consider this passage: "The Pharisees also came to Him, tempting Him, and saying unto Him, 'Is it lawful for a man to put away his wife for every cause?' And He answered and said unto them: 'Have ye not read that he which made them at the beginning made them male and female, and said, "For this cause shall a man leave father and mother, and shall cleave to his wife; and they twain shall be one flesh." Wherefore they are no more twain, but one flesh. What therefore God has joined together let not man put asunder.' They say unto Him, 'Why did Moses then command to give a writing of divorcement, and to put her away?' He saith unto them, 'Moses because of the hardness of your hearts suffered you to put away your wives; but from the beginning it was not so. And I say unto you, "Whosoever shall put away his wife, except it be for fornication, and shall marry another, committeth adultery; and whosoever marrieth her which is put away doth commit adultery."'"[1]

There seems to be little doubt that Christ's ideal of marriage was a monogamous and permanent union. This we should accept not only on religious grounds, but on scientific evidence. The passage just quoted definitely indicates that divorce is far below His ideal. Should we not, however, exercise sympathy, justice and common-sense in the interpretation of individual cases? Christ says: "What therefore God has joined together." Can we honestly say that God could possibly have joined together, or ever wished to join together, some of the people who rush haphazardly into marriage, or have it thrust upon them by social convention and religious demands? Does the fact of being married in church necessarily mean that God has joined the couple together? Is not marriage a willing decision between two people, carefully thought-out and planned? Christ gave us an ideal but He surely expected us to see that those who took on such rigorous responsibilities were adequately prepared for the venture. This is simple sense and justice and is essentially a part of His teaching. A little farther in the same passage He seems to distinguish between types of people and to recognise that some can accept His teaching and others cannot or will not. For them He seems to make allowances; marriage is not for them: "His disciples say unto Him, 'If the case

[1] St. Matthew, Chap. XIX, v. 3–9.

of the man be so with his wife, it is not good to marry'. But He said unto them, 'All men cannot receive this saying, save they to whom it is given. For there are some eunuchs, which were so born from their mother's womb; and there are some eunuchs which were made eunuchs of men; and there be eunuchs, which have made themselves eunuchs for the Kingdom of Heaven's sake. He that is able to receive, let him receive it.'"[1]

That most interesting passage definitely recognises the differences that exist amongst people—even to their biological constitution. We know well that some people are born with a faulty constitution which profoundly affects their physical and emotional life; that others by upbringing or accident or disease are impotent or sterile, while others are celibate of their own volition "for the Kingdom of Heaven's sake".

Christ tempered His judgment with love and understanding. The above passage should teach us not only to tolerate variations from the normal, but to prepare people properly for a venture which requires such a high standard. It might also help us to see the need for a more reasonable code of sexual legislation. Is it right to deny people help on the physical plane when there is so much evidence of marriages failing for this cause? When Christ was confronted by the Pharisees wishing to stone the woman taken in adultery He had understanding and sympathy far greater than those who had accused her.

"He that is without sin among you, let him cast a stone at her."

"And they who heard it, being convicted by their own conscience, went out one by one, beginning at the eldest, even unto the last; and Jesus was left alone, and the woman standing in the midst. When Jesus lifted up himself, and saw none but the woman, he said unto her, 'Woman, where are those thine accusers? Hath no man condemned thee?' She said, 'No man, Lord.' And Jesus said unto her, 'Neither do I condemn thee; go, and sin

[1] St. Matthew, Chap. XIX, v. 10-12.

no more.'"[1] This is not the only time that Christ understood and forgave sexual sins. Indeed, His very understanding and sympathy with all sorts and conditions of women was a source of constant irritation to the Pharisees who were unable to understand His mind or appreciate His insight. His conversation with the woman of Samaria, with whom no good Jew should have spoken because 'Jews have no dealings with Samaritans",[2] is a further example of His understanding of the sexual problem.

Some say that as Christ was unmarried He could not appreciate the difficulties of married people, but this is not borne out by His own sayings and doings, nor does it necessarily follow that a celibate is unable to appreciate these difficulties. Celibate priests are often far more understanding and sympathetic with the practical and psychological difficulties of married couples than married priests or doctors.

These few instances must suffice to indicate the breadth of Christ's understanding of the sexual problem. Perhaps if we realised a little more fully the sympathy He showed in sexual difficulties we should be more willing to bring them to Him, and find out what He has to say about them.

EDUCATION FOR MARRIAGE

Many people reject religious teaching and guidance to-day because of the failure of the Church to tackle the problem of sexual morality in an open and straightforward way. There is something wrong with a religion that allows a girl to decide that she cannot continue her church attendance because she has acquired a young man who presumably kisses her and makes love to her. Yet that is happening all over the country. Young people need help in sexual problems if they are to lead sound lives. Many stay away from the time they first start going about until

---

[1] St. John, Chap. VIII, v. 7–10.
[2] St. John, Chap. IV, v. 9.

they are married, by which time they have lost all faith in religious teaching and cannot see the connection between religion and sex. If the church does not face up to her responsibilities in this matter she will lose her hold on the minds and conduct of the younger generation to an even greater extent than at present. She has a great chance, but it is doubtful if she will take it. So great a change would be required in the outlook of the rank and file of practising church members, that the task seems well-nigh impossible.

If young people are to be married in church it seems only natural that they should be prepared for marriage in church. If our churches are intended for worship they are surely intended for teaching as well. What better place than the church could be found for teaching sex and marriage? The fault is not all on one side. If only young people would understand that their sexual troubles can be brought to God as simply and straightforwardly as any other matter they would find a source of strength which would enable them to think clearly and rationally. Their thinking might show them that their attitude to any particular problem was not in accord with Christ's teaching or modern psychological knowledge, but that might be beneficial. At present they are too apt to think that sex and sin are synonymous. Possibly the following passage in St. Matthew has something to do with this idea: "Whosoever looketh on a woman to lust after her has committed adultery with her already in his heart."[1] This appears to mean that even to think of a woman sexually is wrong, but a careful reading of the passage, together with a knowledge of the psychological principles we have been considering, will help us to a clearer definition. It is necessary to distinguish between the natural and inevitable sexual thoughts which are not sin, and the deliberate imagining and encouragement of the thoughts which are harmful to the individual, unfair to the other person, and definitely wrong. The use of the word lust

[1] St. Matthew, Chap. V, v. 28.

is particularly appropriate in this connection. There is all the difference in the world between looking at a pretty girl and admiring her beauty or her figure, and desiring the girl for herself. There is nothing wrong in the acceptance of the fact of beauty, but there is much to be said against allowing one's imagination full play. Such imaginings are the frequent accompaniment of self-stimulation and if persisted in produce an unhealthy attitude towards women in general.

Self-stimulation after the age of puberty is almost always accompanied by some feeling of guilt or shame or dissatisfaction, which causes the individual to choose a "phantasy object" incapable of being truly loved. His choice falls upon someone who, whilst "not devoid of superficial sexual attractiveness, nevertheless displays some real or supposed inferiority (as regards beauty, virtue, social standing or what not) as a result of which she makes no appeal to the boy's sense of higher moral values. Through frequent repetition of this process women of an inferior type come to be firmly associated with the more directly sexual aspects of love, from which women who are looked upon with tenderness or veneration are correspondingly dissociated, lest these dear objects of affection should be sullied by being brought into contact with what the boy regards as dishonourable, lewd and filthy."[1] Men will often try and rid themselves of their trouble by calling up a vision of a girl they really love. This fact often has repercussions later on when the man marries, because he is unable to rid himself of the feeling that to have a passionate relationship with the girl he really loves and respects is an impossibility. As a result a tension is created in his mind which makes him over-anxious, frequently leading to a hasty performance of the sexual act with accompanying dissatisfaction to both partners.

A true expression of sexual feeling can only occur as a mutual act of love with a person of the opposite sex in which passion plays a most important part.

[1] Professor Flugel, *The Psycho-Analytical Study of the Family*, pp. 111–112

THE FAMILY

Christ was always talking about children and parents and their relationships to each other and constantly illustrated His ideas by reference to the family. His attitude to woman was contrary to the conventional attitude adopted by most strict Jews at that time. Christ neither feared to talk with them nor did He appear to think that they should be segregated; rather did He enter into a real comradeship with them. Here again His actions and teaching receive complete vindication from modern psychology which recognises the paramount importance of a natural relationship between men and women in all spheres of human endeavour.

The more we study the life and teaching of Christ the more do we see the close resemblance between His ideas and those of many modern psychologists, particularly in the sexual sphere. Without over-emphasising the sexual problem, He recognised its importance, and had a far greater understanding of the fundamental needs of men and women than the great majority of those who call themselves His followers. Restrictive and inhuman taboos on sexual knowledge, harsh punishments for sexual offences, and an insistence on a set code of moral behaviour with little psychological backing have often been enforced in utter opposition to His own broad and sympathetic treatment of the whole problem. Indeed, this influence is still strongly felt to-day and forms a dead weight against progressive thought and action. We cannot be altogether surprised at this attitude in early Christian times but we are entitled to ask if it should continue, now that we have much more accurate knowledge of the underlying principles of moral behaviour.

Our moral values must be restated on a synthesis of fundamental Christian teaching, scientific knowledge, and spiritual insight. Christ, who is the master of the art of living, gives us power and understanding with which to develop life on its highest and most perfect level.

CHAPTER III

GROWING UP

> Now some readily receive proper education, while others get no benefit from it. Yet children must not for this reason be neglected, but must be brought up in the best manners. Then, if their nature admits benefit from nurture they will become good men. The management of a child is somewhat like the care of plants. In the latter case no gardener will ever be able to make a bramble-bush bear grapes, since its original nature does not allow of such a consummation. On the other hand, if vines, when ready to bear fruit so to say of their own accord, be neglected and left to nature alone, then they will bear either poor fruit or none at all.
>
> GALEN. 131–201

PHYSICAL GROWTH IS something we can see, but we cannot see the important internal mechanism which brings about the outward change. Most people know that secretions from the ductless glands have an influence on growth but few realise how intimately these secretions are connected with sex life and emotional development.

HORMONES

There are various glands in the body manufacturing chemical substances which pass directly into the blood stream and are called "hormones". The most important of these glands, from our point of view, are the pituitary at the base of the brain, and the sex organs, or gonads. The gonads have two functions; the production of sex cells and the manufacture of hormones. It is possible for one of these functions to cease without disturbing the action of the other. Many otherwise normal men, for instance, do not manufacture sex cells, or sperms, properly, and are often unaware of this deficiency until the matter is inquired into on account of sterility. The only way in which the hormone function can be abolished is by completely removing the primary sex organs, or destroying them by disease. As hormones can travel round in the blood stream, they are capable of influencing organs in different parts of the body. It seems that the director of the ductless glands is the pituitary, the secretions from which regulate the sex glands and others. Indeed, the sex glands cannot manufacture hormones without the initial stimulus from the pituitary.

The influence of the sex hormones on human development has been dealt with at length elsewhere.[1] Suffice it to say that the sex hormones are largely responsible for the production of the sex cells themselves; for the growth and development of the individual from birth, for the changes at puberty, for the maintenance of sexual characteristics and virility, and in particular for emotional development.

There is a close interaction between the various glands which produce a multitude of combinations, and therefore a variety of individuals differing widely in their emotional content. The closest possible relationship exists between the ductless glands and the nervous mechanism of the body. A small area of the brain situated near the pituitary acts as a kind of central telephone exchange. The various impulses necessary for body control come in and go out at this spot and are thus easily influenced by the pituitary and other hormones, as is shown by the sudden response the body can make to reactions such as fear, or anger, which are largely regulated by hormone action.

But growth is neither entirely physical nor entirely emotional. Together with these complicated mechanisms we have a mind, a will and an intelligence, which form our personality and character. A truly balanced individual has to make spiritual adjustments and concerns himself with personal moral principles and also those of the

[1] See *Sex in Everyday Life*, by Edward F. Griffith.

community as a whole. Here again, growth is progressive. Indeed, it is difficult to say when a person has finished growing up. There are so many stages of progress and so many chances of stopping en route. Physical development is almost always accomplished before emotional stability is attained. This is particularly true of men who are not only physically mature, but emotionally sex conscious, long before the personality is really balanced. Women's development is more even; a girl of twenty, for instance, is far more stable physically and emotionally than a man of that age. Failure to recognise these fundamental differences often clouds the personal relationships of young people. Each period of development requires active direction and control if it is to be successfully accomplished.

THE GROWTH OF PERSONALITY

A true development of the personality, which should be the ultimate goal of us all, demands the recognition of many different factors to produce the final balanced result —a well-built physical individual, spiritually alive and emotionally mature.

We have seen that it is necessary to progress from childish self-interest to that comprehensive view-point which embraces thoughtful consideration for the personality of other individuals and, ultimately, the well-being of humanity as a whole. The life-force is the mainspring of this activity. Everything that lives possesses this force, from the simplest cell to the complicated human organism. It is concerned with everything that we do and embraces all the manifestations of life. It incorporates within itself all our various powers, emotions, tendencies, and instincts. Together they ought to form a harmonious whole. We cannot separate bits off and expect them to work by themselves, although we can classify them for purposes of study and discussion. The sex instinct in man, for instance, is part of the greater whole and must be considered as such.

Dc

The tendency to divide off parts of our make-up—especially the sex part—has had disastrous consequences in the past. We must not repeat this. A truly balanced individual has to adjust himself to work, to love and to society. In all this activity the life force is closely allied to the sex drive, indeed many people consider the two forces to be one. Looked at in its narrowest sense sex is merely concerned with physical expression—with reproduction and self-gratification. In its widest sense sex is concerned with the whole well-being of the individual and society. It is concerned with friendship and the development of the family, with love and the development of that team spirit which is essential for co-operation with our fellows. Used, controlled and consciously directed, its beneficial action can free us from the petty self-centred satisfaction of a humdrum existence, raising us to the highest plane of spiritual appreciation. Mishandled and misdirected it can block every creative activity. Thus our attitude to sex will colour our whole outlook on life.

Right motives directing our actions towards ends which are beneficial to the personality are essential for the proper development of character. Too many people never have motives that are of any value to themselves or society. They are utterly self-contained and, unfortunately, often completely self-satisfied. Their lives are devoid of any constructive ideal; they are merely concerned with self-preservation and the avoidance of trouble. Such an individual has shut up half of himself. He has allowed the self to predominate until co-operation with his fellowmen has no place in his life. The same can be said of their sex lives. We all know the type of man and woman whose whole life is centred in sexual variety. Their affairs are designed to stimulate their own emotions and provide some temporary amusement or satisfaction, but there is nothing of lasting value. Here again, self has obtained the upper hand; the broader implications of the sexurge have been avoided.

We cannot altogether blame such people, because

our emotions are constantly being stimulated without being understood or beneficially directed. So much work is dull or monotonous—mentally unproductive—that people have little chance of putting anything of real value into their minds. The mental food of a large proportion of the population consists of a little light literature, newspaper articles in which their thinking is done for them, and emotional fantasies at the cinemas. They are incapable of sustained thought. Now Nature abhors a vacuum, so it fills these minds with trivialities, abnormalities, perversions, ideas of self-importance, immoralities and other evils. One of the difficulties of growing up is the avoidance of these unproductive inconsistencies.

There is all the difference in the world between "suppression" and "repression". We suppress a thing consciously and intentionally, by a definite act of the will. If we repress it, we fail to face the problem, which therefore disappears into the unconscious mind only to reappear in some strange and often highly objectionable form. Ouspensky points out that many people fail to grow up sexually. He terms them "infra-sexed".[1] In these people there is an "absence of co-ordination" between the idea of sex and the other normal functions of man. To them, anything to do with sex is unpleasant and merely a "temptation". A normally sexed individual accepts sex, talks about it naturally when necessary, uses it correctly and happily and therefore fits it naturally into his life. To a man of infra-sex a normal man appears to have some evil force which must be rooted out. Another type of infra-sexed individual is the man who can only find in sex a subject for smutty jokes. Both are really intensely curious about sex but are frightened of it and have never faced up to its meaning or implication in life. They will form unsatisfactory sex partners. They cannot see the strength and beauty that is inherent in the sex relationship. They often become impotent or hasty in their reactions owing to their subconscious feeling that sex is

[1] *A New Model of the Universe*, p. 522.

horrid, only to be enjoyed with a woman of low moral tone and certainly not with one whom one really loves. They are filled with a deep sense of guilt and are therefore unsatisfactory to themselves and everyone else, almost always leaving a trail of unhappiness and misery behind them. They are strangely unappreciative of their real condition and frequently look upon themselves as very fine fellows. Their counterpart is the young woman who drives every man crazy who comes within range of her wiles. Her great delight is to have several on a string at the same time. When matters get too serious she drops them like a stone. She delights in her power of sex attraction and uses it unfairly. Occasionally she is sexually precocious and will have a number of indiscriminate sex relationships in the course of which she destroys the sensibilities of various men and her own into the bargain. In all these cases the individual is self-centred and, of course, anti-social.

These mistaken attitudes to sex are frequently the fault of those responsible for the upbringing of the people concerned. They cannot usually be corrected without the help of someone trained to deal with these problems. A consideration of the processes of psychological development will make this point clearer.

PSYCHOLOGICAL GROWTH

The first essential to proper development is the infant's realisation that it is a person—an ego. As Wexburg clearly puts it: "Great vistas of mental development separate the phrases 'have dolly', 'girlie have dolly' and 'I want my doll'.[1] But this is not all. The child has to realise his own body. This process takes time, requires much experience, and is not complete until adolescence, when the child becomes aware of its own inner life. Adler tells us that the three main experiences of the infant are the feeling of helplessness, of being weaker than adults, and the feeling of dependency on adults. These three together

[1] Erwin Wexburg, *Individual Psychology*, p. 78.

create the consciousness of inferiority which we all possess. From this it naturally follows that we develop a feeling of superiority. This striving for superiority is an attempt to remove the inferiority; it is a compensation.

ORGAN INFERIORITY

Out of this theory of compensation Adler produced his theory of organ inferiority. It is a biological law that weakness in one organ is compensated for by over-activity of a complementary organ. For instance, if an individual loses a kidney through disease the other kidney grows larger and acts more efficiently. Similarly, a diseased heart will grow bigger in an endeavour to compensate for the original weakness. The hearing of one ear becomes more acute if the other is destroyed; the muscles of one limb will over-develop if the other is lost or ineffective. Occasionally over-compensation occurs.

The condition of organ inferiority can be reproduced in the psychological life. Ugliness, fatness, smallness, all create their psychological counterparts. The fat man is usually jolly and good-natured, the ugly one morose or timid and hyper-sensitive. Beauty, too, under certain circumstances can be an organ inferiority. "Beautiful children, admired and spoiled throughout childhood because of their beauty, grow up in the illusion that all they need to do in life is to look pretty. . . . Beauty produces so great a sense of power that it lures the beautiful to repeated tests in the erotic conflicts of the sexes, making them cold-hearted coquettes, interested only in subjugating their sexual partners. . . . The Don Juan who loves women only as a hunter loves his prey is a product of this thirst for power that grows from misused beauty."[1]

Similarly, inferiority of the sex organs, either supposed or real, may have disastrous consequences on the future life. Some minor defect in a boy is often translated in his mind into a serious disorder which may make him grow

[1] E. Wexburg, *Individual Psychology*, p. 134.

up with such a feeling of inferiority that he avoids the whole question and becomes clumsy and tongue-tied in the presence of women. It may even cause him to lead a sexless life. Deficiencies in the development of the secondary sexual characteristics may have an equally inhibiting effect. The boy who possesses strong feminine traits, or the masculine type of girl, may feel themselves to be so abnormal that they avoid normal friendships and experiences with members of the opposite sex.

This natural feeling of inferiority, which we all possess in some degree, may utterly transform the life and character of an individual, if it is not compensated by the natural development of the feeling of superiority. The desire to achieve and overcome obstacles is the natural reaction of the child to this situation. Success leads to satisfaction and self-esteem. Every experience has to be reckoned as a gain or a loss.

We make progress in various ways; by imitation, for instance, or by training. It is by such means that we learn to walk. As we progress the action becomes easier, more reflex in character, until eventually we walk without conscious effort save in the original determination. The purpose has been achieved, the desired goal—an ability to walk as others walk—satisfactorily reached. But the personal will has to act even so; there must be a conscious purposive willing to walk. We walk, and learn, and achieve all manner of things because we have a goal. If we have no goal we have no desire, no push. We become lazy and indolent. We must have faith in ourselves and motive in our life. As these words were being written, Lord Elton's voice came over the wireless. "You can do what you believe you can do." He added that this is one of the profoundest laws of life. How right he is!

PLAY

The capacity for achievement is fostered by our ability to play. Childhood games train us in responsibility, discipline and communal activities. They fit us to take our place in society; to rub shoulders with other people and take knocks. But even here there is a danger. We must learn to grow out of our play-phase. We must direct our play towards a goal.

We need not only faith in ourselves, but courage to become independent, self-reliant, and strong, the opposites of the three constituents of inferiority—helplessness, weakness, and dependence. By the development of these positive qualities we obtain a sense of security and self-reliance.

Play has a further use in that it enables us to co-operate with our fellow-beings, which is essential if we are to live fully and richly, because our ability to live in happy communion with our fellow men is the essence of life itself. Man was never intended to live alone. No one is self-sufficient. Our functions may differ but our unity and co-operation is essential. "Civilisation and culture," Wexburg tells us, "are the products of communal life." We inherit much from our ancestors and the sum of the knowledge and learning that we so inherit is automatically grafted on to ourselves. We term this accumulation of knowledge "social feeling".

SOCIAL FEELING

We can either live in partnership with others, or we can live as parasites. The child is at first a parasite, totally dependent on others and has to learn the art of social reciprocity. He does this by becoming independent and overcoming inferiority. The more confidence he gains the more easily can he take his rightful place in the community. The greater the social feeling the greater is the capacity for co-operation. If the child grows properly his social feeling will develop naturally. The aim of true education should be to develop it.

Many modern problems are the outcome of a deficiency in this social feeling. Many of the undesirable people in our midst, and we have a "social problem group", of about four million, are the direct result of bad economic conditions, faulty education, and childhood deprivations which have developed those character traits diametrically opposed to true social feeling. Criminals, drunkards, and prostitutes war on society because their psychological pattern has been moulded that way in childhood. Poverty, dirt, slums, and economic insufficiency batten on the child and magnify its feeling of inferiority until its whole purpose in life is to get those things which it has lacked—quiet, security, ease, and pleasure. Selfish ends no doubt, but easily understandable in the light of the misery through which it has passed in its early years. Of course this is not the whole picture. There is the hereditary constitution to be thought of, as well as the environment. But if love and tenderness are not present in the home; if there is no possibility for emotional expression, the child will grow up afraid of showing emotion or tenderness, for fear of being ridiculed. He will withdraw into a shell of isolation.

On the other hand, an excess of tenderness, which dissolves into petting, is equally disastrous because the child is kept away from responsibility and given no chance to act on its own initiative. "Such children are utterly unprepared for life because they have never had an opportunity to practise the conquest of difficulties."[1]

SEX

The adjustment that the individual makes in the sexual sphere is of equal importance to those which he makes in work and society. In many ways it is a more difficult one. It is intensely personal and essentially social in the sense that it involves another person and also society as a whole. It is indeed part of the social task of the individual. If he expresses it in marriage and the creation of a family he will be expressing it in a socially beneficial manner. If he keeps it to himself, or exercises his powers in an egocentric

[1] Adler, *Understanding Human Nature*, p. 40.

or self-seeking manner he will be acting anti-socially and against his own best interest. He will certainly not be working to full capacity.

The mating instinct is strangely compelling and highly complex. It is possible that the desire for sex union is developed before that of reproduction. It can scarcely be said that it is the desire for children that first brings two people together. The desire for reproduction and family responsibility is the final stage in a long developmental progress, which must be reached before we can be considered as truly adult-minded and fully conscious of our social responsibilities. Many people never reach this state; their physical growth has outstripped their emotional development; whilst others have the situation forced upon them before they are well able to carry out the responsibilities which the position demands. As a result they break down either physically or psychologically, and become prematurely old or remain emotionally underdeveloped. The economic conditions under which they have to bring up their children are often too much for the parents, so that they remain permanently immature, more so, in fact, than the children whom they bring into the world. Nevertheless, the very fact of becoming pregnant develops a woman to a remarkable extent, just as the added responsibility develops the man.

As there are stages of emotional growth from parasites to parental independence and full social feeling, so is there sexual growth from self-interest and sex-play to interest in the opposite sex and desire for sex union, leading eventually to the full development of social feeling and responsibility in family life and corporate activity. As development in one sphere may stop at an intermediate stage, so can sex development stop at sex union and never progress to the stage of family or corporate life. It may stop even earlier. Many a full-grown man is still in his infantile stage and is interested in self-stimulation instead of in the fullest development of his sex life.

IMAGINATION

Many children live almost entirely in a world of fantasy, and the process of growing up consists largely in relating fantasy to everyday life; something that we so frequently fail to do. The fully grown man who is interested in self-stimulation rather than in a fully matured sex life derives most of his pleasure from imaginative fantasies. Imagination can be used beneficially or otherwise. It can become creative or self-centred. We can no more avoid the play of our imagination than we can avoid sex thoughts. They are both normal healthy attributes. Nevertheless, we undoubtedly make our sex lives more or less difficult by the way we deal with our imagination. Fantastic day-dreaming is a stage through which young adolescents should quickly pass; girls in particular often go through a phase of romantic day-dreaming in which their imaginations are allowed so much freedom that they frequently land themselves in serious situations through inability to distinguish between imagination and reality. They clothe a friendship with a romantic glamour which is outside the realm of possibility, demanding more than the other individual is prepared to give, or refusing to see any shortcomings he or she may possess. They create in their minds an "ideal man", who is either a combination of all the virtues that they find in their fathers and brothers, or a development of those ideal qualities they find lacking in their relatives. This "ideal" individual is added to and made even more attractive by the romantic stories they read. As a result, the first man who pays them any attention is endowed with all these attributes. A girl will go to almost any lengths to preserve the friendship and illusion that she has built up in her imagination regarding such a man.

SELF-CONTROL

The term is largely misused, particularly in the sexual sphere where it is confused with repression. If self-control in the sexual sphere means denying the possession of a sexual urge; that the very thoughts that come into our minds are wrong and bad in themselves; that sexual pleasure is sinful and base, then there is something wrong with the individual. The sex instinct is no better or worse than any other instinct. All can be used beneficially or abused. The value that we put on them will largely determine our attitude towards them. If we misuse them we have no right to blame them; the fault is in ourselves.

If self-control does not mean repression, neither does it mean expression. Those who are always trying to "express" themselves are no more facing up to the conditions of life than those who refuse to admit there is such a thing as passion.

The man who is always smoking or drinking, or going to the races, is using part of himself to excess; and the same applies to the fellow who is always reading or attending to his job and has no time for anything else. Moderation is a most valuable asset. This does not mean that we should never enjoy ourselves, but we should not allow anything to become a habit that we cannot stop. A balanced individual allows to all his emotions and feelings that measure of expression that is good for them. The cinema operator whose occupation on his evening off is to take his girl to the pictures has a one-track mind which will never enable him fully to develop his personality. On the other hand, inability to concentrate and stick to a job is one of the worst curses of our age.

It is possible to make a success of the most unlikely occupations, but it needs decision and staying power. But even the decisions may be escapes from reality. It is so easy to change a job because one is fed up; to go out and be gay instead of staying in to work for an exam.

If one always takes the easier path all desire to progress is eventually lost. All the initiative and creative ability evaporate.

We have to teach ourselves to make constructive decisions. Hesitation and vacillation will achieve nothing. Whilst we try to make up our minds, the job will have gone to another. If we have made a mistake we should cut our losses and start again, but impulsiveness unaccompanied by reason is fatal.

No effort that is worth anything will be made without a positive goal. What is our sexual goal? If it is love and devotion to another rather than self-satisfaction we must exercise considerable control to achieve it. We will not do this unless we are really satisfied that what we are doing is right. This brings us back to a consideration of motive. There is a difference between the primary motive which is a natural biological force, and may be termed desire, and the end motive which, in its highest manifestation, is love.

THE RE-DIRECTION OF SEX ENERGY

The re-direction of this primary force is of the utmost importance, more especially for the young adult male, who naturally finds the management of his sex feelings a serious difficulty. The difficulty occurs in women, too, if not perhaps in such a pronounced form. But there are numberless young women who, for one reason or another, find it difficult to obtain emotional release and are frequently thrust back upon themselves. Society is still largely to blame by insisting that women must repress emotions.

The principle underlying the re-direction of this energy is that it must be translated to a plane where it does good to other people and ultimately to society. We must fill our minds with productive thoughts, regulate our conduct along positive lines, and direct our energies into useful channels. We are doing this to a greater or less degree all day long. We do it whether we are single or married.

To do it properly it may be necessary to change the whole pattern of life, and to give up friends who have a bad influence. But this is just what so many people won't do. They are happy in their unproductive amusements and enjoy fantastic day-dreams. If only they would realise that there is joy and satisfaction to be found in working for other people, their sense of frustration would disappear in productive activity.

Thousands of young people are condemned to a monotonous routine which fails to provide them with adequate mental and physical satisfaction, and leaves them dissatisfied and tired. They seek relief and forgetfulness in emotional sensation. It is vitally important for such people to make the effort to find constructive occupations such as can be obtained in youth movements, scouts, and girl-guides, clubs and out-door activities. Among the more intellectual pursuits, there are a variety of professions which will provide opportunity for creative activity. Engineering, medicine, and the legal professions, art, music, and literature, all provide possibilities for creative work beneficial both to the individual and to society.

The individual may still find it difficult to lead an emotionally balanced and tranquil life. One of the best ways to regulate the emotions is by having a satisfactory comradeship with someone of the opposite sex in which the personality of both is fully respected. And if our sexual thoughts persist, it is advisable to try and avoid the situations which produce the initial stimulus. It is no use trying to deal with a strong emotional situation when in its grip. Wait until the feeling has passed off, try and decide how to act in the future, and then make a conscious effort of will to carry out that decision. This often means altering the train of thought or changing the occupation. From a physiological point of view sexual feeling appears to vary in intensity at different times in both men and women. That it does so in women is well recognised now, but there is evidence that such a sexual rhythm exists in men also, although its functioning has not been clearly

worked out. Some men can discover their own rhythm
or cycle. It should not be impossible, therefore, for an
individual to reduce possible sources of stimulation to a
minimum at such times.

Some people argue that because sex energy rises and
falls in this physiological way—because the "psychologists"
say that the instincts should be expressed and not bottled
up, sexual energy should be satisfied when the desire for
expression arises, in the same way as hunger must be
satisfied. Here, however, they are on insecure ground.
The sex instinct can only be rightfully expressed in
co-operation with one of the opposite sex. The hunger
instinct can only be expressed individually.

Secondly, the sex instinct, according to Freud, possesses
the ability to displace its aim without materially losing
its intensity. The original sexual aim can be exchanged
for another closely related to it but on a higher level of
consciousness. This is the meaning of sublimation. The
realisation of this principle is one of the major necessities of
life. The hunger instinct cannot be dealt with in this manner.

Thirdly, the mind can exercise a strong controlling
influence over the whole physiological system. The
instinctive drives are, from a psychological point of view,
controlled and regulated by a higher function of the
personality which Freud has termed the "super ego".
"In the ideal personality there should be no conflict in
this process, for all the instincts will develop in a harmonious
manner, so that they are raised from their crude state to
their finished products, which are to the highest degree
useful to the individual and the community."[1]

The main danger in our lives to-day is mental and
spiritual stagnation. From the moment we get up to the
moment we go to bed we live artificially. Our homes are
run on labour-saving principles; our food is partially
prepared before it even comes into the house; we work
in an artificial atmosphere, at unproductive or monotonous
occupations. We amuse ourselves by watching others play

[1] Gordon, Harris and Rees, *Introduction to Psychological Medicine*, p. 85.

games or by switching on the wireless. When we leave the towns we sit at the road-side to eat our lunch or crowd together on beaches. We are afraid of solitude, peaceful occupations, a country lane, or our own thoughts. We are consumed with a crazy desire for movement and still more movement. And for what end? We seem to be driven relentlessly by powers beyond our comprehension and control: by principles based on the love of power, the desire for self-aggrandisement and self-seeking.

Now that we are at war these feelings are intensified. It is difficult to find any purpose in life when a bomb may drop on one at any moment. War creates a tendency to let things slide; to enjoy oneself without giving much thought to others. Such an aimless life, devoid of purpose, leads to a sterile personality—a useless member of society. Creative ideals, energy, and enthusiasm for the benefit of society are frittered away.

We must learn to accept a new conception of our purpose on earth by realising that we shall never save ourselves by gratifying ourselves. We must keep to this ideal even in the fog of war and death. We must live in the hope of creating something better out of present chaos. That is precisely why we are at war. This does not rule out enjoyment—that would be senseless, but it does require us to give consideration to others in our enjoyment. It also demands that we think farther ahead than the next twenty-four hours. We must think in terms of mankind and train ourselves for what Mr. Zilliacus calls "world citizenship".[1]

For this, according to Sir Ernest Simon, we require four main principles:—

1. A sense of social responsibility.
2. A love of truth and freedom.
3. The power of clear thinking in everyday affairs.
4. A knowledge of the political and economic facts of the modern world.

To these Mr. Zilliacus adds a fifth:—a practical ability in the duties and task of citizenship. We venture to add a sixth:—a sense of sex equality.

---

[1] "Education for World Citizenship" in *Education To-day*.

It is easy to see how these principles, if applied to the problem of sexual morality in its largest sense, would have a productive influence on our social structure. The sense of social responsibility would prevent us from using the sex urge in a negative or selfish fashion. We would realise the value of children to the community, and would insist on their proper education and upbringing; and on the development of natural mental capacity, irrespective of their social or economic position. We would take steps to regulate the present anti-social trends in population production; the excessive breeding of unsuitable stocks, and the under-production of those whose mental and cultural capacity is likely to be of value to the community. We would stress the importance of education for citizenship, realising that all these educational efforts will come to naught while the physical and mental qualities of the children are deteriorating. The love of truth and freedom would teach us the value of human personality whilst the power of clear thinking would enable us to regulate our conduct on rational lines. Finally, a sense of sex equality would broaden our outlook and make us live as responsible citizens respecting the personalities of those around us.

CHAPTER IV

FRIENDSHIP

People whose sentiments, and particularly whose tastes correspond, naturally like to associate together, although neither of them have the most distant view of any further connection. But, as this similarity of minds often gives rise to a more tender attachment than friendship, it will be prudent to keep a watchful eye over yourselves, lest your hearts become too far engaged before you are aware of it.

JOHN GREGORY. 1723–1773

FRIENDSHIP POSSESSES SO many facets that it is really indefinable. Community of interests in work or play, a liking for the arts or literature, a love of exercise and the out-of-doors; a delight in the company and occupation of another, his conversation, his silly habits, his desire to do things for one—with one; of such are true friendships made. Friendship often makes heavy demands on our time and patience, but it brings out the best in us. The threads of an old friendship can often be gathered after years of absence. There is a quality about true friendship which exists in no other relationship—not even in love. It is steadier and less likely to burn away with emotional heat or wither from lack of attention. It may start as an instinctive mutual attraction, or it may grow through a community of interests. Once started it does not grow automatically any more than marriage or religion. Something must be *done* about it. Nothing in life just "comes".

No one person is completely satisfying to another. As the personality grows new shoots appear which in their turn form further attachments so that our circle of friendship and interest is ever widening. The more friends we make, within reason, the more we shall be able to give to the friendships we have already made. A practical point of view of some importance arises here. Whilst it is natural and right that we should extend our sphere of friendship, it may happen that we may meet someone to whom we are immediately attracted physically, and the attraction may be mutual. Are we to allow the friendship to take its course, and possibly become entangled in a complicated emotional relationship, or are we to draw back? Two considerations should help us. We have numerous satisfactory friendships and probably one person to whom we are emotionally attached by engagement or marriage. Will the new relationship spoil something that we already possess and value? If so, we must retreat, frankly admitting the new physical attraction but recognising that we have already responsibilities and duties which must not be disturbed. Secondly, what effect will the new relationship have on the other individual?

Ec

If the emotional attraction can be removed or overcome there is no reason why the friendship should not progress along ordinary lines. If it cannot, it should be brought to an end, because it is obvious that it could not develop without disturbing the other personality. Many unfortunate situations would be avoided if people would exercise a little more control over the conduct prompted by their early reactions.

An individual is not properly adjusted to society until he can make a variety of friendships. Some friendships are so perfect that they are akin to love, but they are not of the same type as love, which demands physical expression. Many friendships could never work as marriages. There is a particular quality, essentially necessary, but difficult to define, which distinguishes love from friendship. Whilst not entirely physical, its roots lie in the physical. On the other hand, many young people are mistakenly afraid of admitting the physical into friendship. If it comes it must be dealt with openly and constructively. It may be that the relationship is to develop into love; if so, it should not be thwarted. On the other hand love may not be possible; perhaps one partner does not feel the same physical attraction as the other. In this case a refusal to face the situation will only make matters worse.

FRIENDSHIP AND LOVE

Friendship embraces mutual understanding and interest, affinity, co-operation and self-sacrifice, without the strong physical attachment that is present in love. Friendship is the essential basis of marriage, which is a union of mutually adjusted personalities striving for creative companionship and happiness. It is a progressive building of which the wedding is but the first brick. The foundation rests on mutual compatibility and a certain harmony of character that will enable a couple to meet and circumvent the difficulties which are bound to arise. It may not be necessary to like and do the same things, but it is necessary to have the same pattern of life, to attach the same meaning and value to the fundamentals of behaviour; to be tuned in on the same wave-length.

An underlying current of antagonism, difficult to define but easily recognisable, is a danger signal that should not be ignored. Such character traits as a deeply ingrained self-centredness or possessiveness can only be discovered by knowing a person really well. Hence the importance of making friendship the foundation of marriage. No couple is so perfectly matched that they cannot learn more about each other; that they will not have to give and take, with willingness and mutual understanding. It is vitally important that they should be able to talk to each other; that they should not bottle up or gloss over difficulties, only to bring them out in a moment of anger.

Given the same system of values; the same principles; intuition, understanding, and willingness to co-operate, and make a success of the job, combined with physical compatibility, most couples could make marriage a success. The completed structure, however, will take years in the building. This is what so many young people will not realise. They expect marriages to be turned out ready made by a benevolent God much in the same way that their furniture or the wireless set is produced ready for use. At the first sign of trouble they turn and fly or give up the job in disgust and despair. Any personal relationship must be forged and tested before it is properly tempered.

Friendship, therefore, as well as love is essential to marriage. Friendship forms the rock upon which the emotional element in love can play in safety. In the last analysis there is little difference between the two, because both have their final expression in self-sacrifice for the other, for the cause or for the community, even to death.

EQUALITY OR DOMINATION

Not until we recognise the meaning of sex equality will real friendship between the sexes become possible. At present we are brought up to believe that man is superior to woman; that to be masculine is to be virile, to be feminine is to be weak. Traditions, laws and customs all protect male privilege. The father is the symbol of power. Man has achieved his position owing to his ability to fight. As a result he has acquired property and "rights" both of which give him power. There are no psychological grounds for his superiority, indeed every man has a large feminine element and every woman a masculine element and both must be accepted and used. But to the girl there appear to be many advantages in being a man. All the best things in life seem to belong to the dominant male—positions, titles, victories and honour. And yet these manly qualities are mainly self-centred and egoistic. Man is no better at bearing pain than woman, indeed he is far more difficult to nurse. Men have less resistance than women to illness or infection. Women have as great an aptitude for the professions and arts as men. In courage, patience and endurance women can outdo men. Indeed, in many ways women are superior. They are more faithful in friendship, forbearing in adversity and forgiving in love. It must be admitted also that they may be more violent in hatred, more possessive in their love.

Many women never "do" anything simply because they have never been encouraged to do or think for themselves. They have been told for so long that their place is only in the home that they have come to believe it. In actual fact many are capable of managing both home and business, which is more than can be said for many men. A change of outlook on the part of the male sex is long overdue. Male dominance must go. Only when they enjoy true equality in business and pleasure will women be able to make a real adjustment to life, because only then will they possess a real sense of security. When equality of personality and difference of function is admitted and respected, women will cease to be dissatisfied with the feminine role. We shall cease to see women endeavouring to evade their feminine responsibilities by adopting a masculine outlook to compensate for the supposed deficiencies of their own sex. Those women who possess a "masculine response" often avoid love and marriage in the belief that they are superior, or they go to the opposite extreme and become so resigned, obedient, humble and helpless that they are totally unfitted for social life.

ADOLESCENT FRIENDSHIPS

Adolescence is a time of strong and varying emotional stresses. We frequently come across people who seem wholly delightful and with whom we feel we could well spend the rest of our life, only to find that after a few weeks or even days our hero or heroine, being human, is, after all, imperfect. As a result a coolness sets in. Such experiences are natural and, as long as they are recognised for what they are, can do no harm. There should be no recriminations when the friendship is dropped; that too is natural. We learn by a system of trial and error.

Many adolescent friendships will come to a natural end largely because physical and emotional development by no means necessarily go hand in hand. Jung tells us that a youth of marriageable age has only just started to emerge from "the mist of original unconsciousness". He is only "imperfectly informed as to the motives of others and of himself. As a rule he acts almost entirely from unconscious motives".[1]

Calf love and hero worship are perfectly right in moderation and should be respected. The emotions stirred up and the heart-rendings when things go wrong are just as strong and painful at sixteen as at twenty-five; more so in fact, because they are less well understood. Young

[1] Jung, *Marriage*. Contribution to *Analytical Psychology*.

teachers, in particular, should be understanding and sympathetic to the expressions of affection and friendship showered on them by their pupils. When it is necessary to draw the line this should be done carefully and considerately. It is a great mistake to accept presents from youthful admirers. Hero worship is a normal condition of development and can be used by an intelligent elder to further the creative activities of the younger person by providing encouragement and a goal at which to aim. It can be misused if it is allowed too free expression and is not related to reason and common sense.

There is a particular danger of allowing the strong emotional feeling to develop into actual physical expression. Such a situation may arise between teacher and child of the same sex or between a man and a young girl. Believing in the good faith of the elder the girl will often surrender to his will and develop a disastrous relationship.

Adolescent friendships should be based on common interests and mutual respect like more mature relationships. Young people are extremely sensible if only things are properly explained to them. They are also intensely responsive to creative suggestions. The main criterion on which any friendship must be judged is the amount of giving that enters into the relationship. Not one-sided giving but mutual giving. Not the giving of presents but the giving of self; the sharing of the self with the other.

EMOTIONAL FRIENDSHIPS

Closely allied to this problem is that of emotional friendships between young people of the same age and sex. One of the unsatisfactory results of our system of segregated education is that an emotional friendship between two boys or two girls is frequently treated as a serious evil by the authorities. Such things simply "aren't done". But there is no reason why they shouldn't be done, indeed the whole moral tone of a school would probably be greatly improved if these friendships were openly recognised and respected by the teachers and understood by the pupils. The danger of them becoming so pronounced as to exclude other friendships could usually be averted by a short explanation of the principles involved. Children must have an emotional outlet; if they do not get it naturally they feel frustrated and tend to become introspective and develop unsatisfactory sexual habits, such as self-stimulation. The fear that such friendships may become "unhealthy" and lead to mutual stimulation would be minimised if the children were given simple explanations of the physical and psychological development they were undergoing. [1]

POSSESSIVE FRIENDSHIPS

Some friendships, especially among women, are far too possessive. One partner expects the other to give up all or most of her other friends and occupations. One character in such a relationship dominates the other by the strength and force of her personality. If she cannot make her friend do as she wants by persuasion she resorts to unfair methods, pretending to be ill or lonely or unhappy, to keep the weaker character attached to her. Or a man will expect his fiancée to give up her friends and amusements and spend all her time with him, accepting all his friends and adopting his activities. Such relationships are most unhealthy, and usually indicate that the dominant partner suffers from some fear or disharmony which makes a normal social life impossible for him or her. The same occurs in marriage. If persisted in, the one becomes more and more domineering while the other becomes cringing and submissive. It is not natural for people to be entirely wrapped up in each other in this manner. Each one of us needs a variety of friends from whom to receive, and to whom to give, benefits.

All friendships cannot be expected to last, or to remain on the same basis. Some do, but others, which were

[1]See Chapter IX for a further discussion on this problem.

delightfully satisfying at eighteen, are incapable of develop-ment and come to an end fairly quickly.

Neither does friendship necessarily involve bodily surrender. It is unfair of a man to expect a girl to exhibit physical feeling towards him merely on the strength of common interests. Of course the physical may come into the relationship, but many people are firmly united in friendship on account of a piece of mutual work. If the physical comes into the affair it is only good if it refreshes and strengthens both partners.

We get different things from different people. Friendship should expand, not restrict, the personality. One person satisfies certain traits in our character whilst another appeals to an entirely different side. Men are naturally friendly with a variety of men, and there is no reason why they should not be friendly with a variety of women. Similarly, women have numerous women friends and there is no reason why they should not have numerous men friends.

HUSBANDS AND WIVES

Some people think that husbands and wives should be sufficient to each other. Most couples would be happier and more interesting if each had friends from whom to draw inspiration and encouragement. Marriages can be greatly enriched by such friendships, but responsibility, frankness and trust are essential if a marriage is to work well under such conditions. Jealousy must be unknown. It may be asked whether such freedom will not lead to trouble simply because husbands and wives will meet people to whom they will be physically attracted. This is perfectly true, but the answer applies here that has been made all along, namely that the way to develop character is by a healthy mixing of the sexes in a spirit of mutual understanding and respect, backed by knowledge.

There is no harm in being attracted. The important point is to learn to manage the affair sensibly and without hurting anyone.

PHYSICAL EXPRESSION IN FRIENDSHIP

Equality is essential if friendship between the sexes is to mean anything vital. Only by mixing the sexes shall we obtain real understanding and respect. Only by this means will men come to view women from another angle than that of mere sexuality. This is not to say that men are not different from women or will not be attracted by them. Of course they will. Indeed, most youthful friendships have an emotional content which should be recognised. So long as the physical does not over-reach itself no harm will be done. The difficulty is to keep the relationship within bounds. Emotions have a habit of boiling over, especially if their presence is not willingly admitted and frankly discussed. Their energy must be properly directed and physical expression must be limited to minor contacts which should not be prolonged and should be mutually satisfactory. This can only be done if each wishes to do the best for the other. It is not suggested that people should not kiss and flirt in moderation, but such behaviour should be part of a relationship constructive in outlook and not a mere physical stimulation. Knowledge of physical facts and possible dangers is essential, as is a willingness to face facts, and the adoption of a mode of life which will minimise the physical and yet give sufficient emotional relief.

Avoid a drifting policy. Is the relationship to develop into an engagement or not? If not, bring it to an end, without recrimination. It is far better to face a situation than to pretend it does not exist. If the man will not take the initiative in clearing up the situation the woman should. The initial advances are usually made by the man, but it is not at all necessary for a woman to be aloof and coy. If she likes a man she should let him know it. Similarly a woman should realise that if a man constantly takes her out he is probably attracted, and if she does not reciprocate his feelings she should let the man know. It is unfair to keep a person dangling at the end of an emotional string. There is nothing shameful in liking a person or in being liked. Indeed, it is a compliment. If it is impossible to return the compliment this should be made plain by a frank talk.

An engaged couple must decide how much physical expression can be allowed into their relationship. Some emotional expression is essential, but it should not dominate the situation. There should be a feeling of mental well-being, and contentment, after any physical expression of love. If the opposite results the relationship is probably wrong.

PETTING PARTIES

Petting parties are most unsatisfactory. They cause a serious charging up of the emotional mechanism without providing effective relief. This is physically and psychologically bad. Most petting parties seem to be run on the principle that a man can go as far as a girl will let him, or that a girl may egg a man on and arouse his desires to breaking point without any intention of allowing him free rein. Such an adventure is often embarked upon out of curiosity or bravado.

It may be satisfactory to a girl who knows herself to be pretty and attractive, to captivate a man; it may give her a sense of power and satisfy some primitive craving for possession, but it is intensely cruel. The last thing she is willing to do is to permit actual intimacy. If she persists in this behaviour she will eventually become a callous little beast. However, the fault is not all on her side. There is an equally repulsive type of young man—he is worse when he is old—who makes a habit of seeing how far he can go with a girl. A past master of the ancient art of seduction, he is utterly selfish, frightened at the first suggestion of exposure, and an expert at escaping from a nasty situation. Such a man can drive girls distracted, although he is soon spotted by women of more mature experience. If a girl is well grounded in positive principles, she need not be frightened by such a man. The best way of dealing with a drunken man is to hit him hard in the middle of his chest. The best way to deal with a cad is to stand up to him and threaten exposure.

THE EMOTIONAL BASIS

One fact that young people do not seem to realise is that constant stimulation of the emotions, which cannot end in complete relaxation, creates a tension in one or both, which may be very harmful. The normal proces of love-making consists, from a physiological point of view, in a gradual charging up of the sex organs, which eventually leads to a state of tension that is relieved by coitus. Most people realise that a large proportion of the blood can be transferred from one part of the body to another as required. For instance, the process of digestion necessitates the concentration of the blood in the digestive organs. Intense mental concentration demands a similar distribution of blood to the brain, and sex activity demands more blood in the sex organs. The engorgement is relieved by the completion of the sex act. This process occurs in women in precisely the same way as in men. If it is continually taking place without appropriate relief the organs eventually become over-charged, and, as the mechanism of discharge is not allowed to work properly, they may become damaged. As sex intercourse cannot occur whenever one feels inclined, it is necessary to regulate oneself so that the tension does not become too great.

Quite apart from these physical problems, psychological manifestations have to be taken into account. People who are always exciting themselves emotionally develop psychological inhibitions, which may cause considerable difficulty when they enter into a proper sex relationship. The main objective is the achievement of a balanced relationship in which the physical does not obtrude itself unnecessarily. This does not rule out some physical expression, but it does limit it to that measure which is beneficial.

Each couple has to work out a method of behaviour which,
whilst not being ideally perfect, is essentially practical and
useful. They have to decide to go so far and no farther;
to devote a quarter of an hour to physical intimacies rather
than the whole afternoon. If the reason is apparent the
solution should not prove too difficult.

CHAPTER   V

PRINCIPLES OF SEX RELATIONSHIPS

> A physical fact is as sacred as a moral principle. Our own
> nature demands from us this double allegiance.
>
> LOUIS AGASSIZ. 1807-1873

We ARE NOW in a position to enumerate some of
the principles upon which sex relationships should be
based. Let us first of all recapitulate some of the factors
which are *not* conducive to the formation of a positive
sex ethic.

NEGATIVE FACTORS

1. We must repudiate the suggestion that the sex urge
is in any way sinful. On the contrary it is God-given and
positive.

To say, for instance; "In sin did my mother conceive
me" in the sense often attributed to the words, is to make
a statement diametrically opposed to everything we know
and believe concerning the meaning and nature of sex.
It suggests that, even in marriage, sex relationships are
wrong and gives countenance to the argument that it is an
institution primarily intended for the satisfaction of our
baser needs. It has been suggested that this phrase does not
mean that the sex act in marriage is sinful; that it is a
misreading of the context to regard it as such. Nevertheless,
the majority of people do look upon it as meaning that

there is something sinful about the reproductive process and it is this interpretation that we wish to combat.

2. That the management of the sex urge depends upon fear of punishment, either in this world or the next, is far short of the ideal. People react to fear in two main ways. The immediate reaction may be a positive one, which is concerned with the removal or avoidance of the condition causing the fear; a defence reaction, for instance, in the case of a man who jumps over a five-barred gate in order to escape from a bull. Here the fear sets free strong emotional forces, which are directed towards a positive purpose—the safety of the individual. The other way fear can act is negatively in which the situation is not squarely faced but is avoided and repressed. There is no control or positive direction of energy. The control exercised by religion over sexual behaviour in the past has been based largely on this second method.

For instance, some people say that self stimulation may lead to impotence or madness or that sexual union outside marriage produces venereal disease and so on. That is incorrect. Of course it is right to have a healthy fear of venereal disease but that one's whole attitude to these problems should be regulated by this negative approach merely means the production of a poor timid creature afraid of himself and everybody else. There is no positive direction in his life; no true discipline—merely repression and avoidance of the issue. It would be far better for this control to be exercised through reason. It is impossible to manage anything satisfactorily unless it is understood. Sex power has been feared because it has not been understood. Such regulation as has been possible has been made by men who lacked the knowledge we possess to-day.

3. Any sense of guilt or shame regarding the creative use of sex is quite untenable. A moral code based upon outworn rules and laws which owe their origin to fear, magic and taboo, rather than to intelligence and reason, is no longer worthy of the support of intelligent and free people. Indeed, its abolition is long overdue.

Any use of the sex urge that is contrary to the fundamental laws of our being must raise up feelings of remorse
and guilt. But the "fundamental laws" on which most
moral issues are judged to-day are based on false premises
and are therefore suspect. A man who impregnates a
woman and abandons her and her child is acting against
a fundamental law. There is nothing to be found in support
of such behaviour in biological, sociological or ethical
history. His action, being socially destructive, is fundamentally wrong, and must raise up guilty feelings in his
mind. Whether or not he recognises these feelings they
must inevitably arise, unless he is of low or subnormal
intelligence, in which case he is not a responsible member
of society, and should not be given the chance of behaving
in such a manner.

Or take the case of a man who impregnates a woman
and marries her without love because society demands
that he shall "make a good woman of her". He takes vows
of ›life-long devotion and fidelity that are manifestly
impossible to keep, because society and "the Church"
demand it. The social conscience is appeased by such
behaviour. But the swearing of oaths and the signing of
a register will not alter the attitude of this man and woman.
Their union is fundamentally wrong. Very soon one, or
both, will find a true mate—or at least a more likely mate.
Does society sanction the second union? Not a bit of it.
One of the partners has committed adultery. So the other
can sue for divorce. Should both commit adultery, however,
neither can be divorced—they are tied together indissolubly.
Society says that they have committed sin, whereas the
sin lies with society, for allowing people to grow up with
so little sense of responsibility that the original relationship
was permitted, and further for permitting such an unsatisfactory marriage.

Again, take the case of a woman who leaves her husband
because his behaviour to her and her child makes life
impossible for her and bad for the child. She puts herself
in the wrong at once by leaving him, although his behaviour

may be the cause of her troubles. This is grossly unfair. If he divorces her he obtains custody of the child, however unfitted he may be for that responsibility. If he refuses to divorce her or give her cause for divorce, she is tied to him for ever. How barbaric! How utterly un-Christian! She has no redress, and yet he has failed in his duty both to wife and child. Does the wife's duty lie with the man who has ruined her life or with the child whose life, at present unspoilt, will be warped by such a man? She can, of course, obtain a separation but this is hardly likely to be a satisfactory solution and condemns the woman to a celibate existence or encourages her to have some unsatisfactory liaison. Would it not be wiser to have prevented the original marriage or at least to have given some preliminary help or guidance? Would it not be in the interest of parent, child, and society if the future custody of the child were decided upon factors other than those of matrimonial infidelity? It by no means follows that because a woman commits adultery and the man does not, that he is really fitted to look after the child.

The trouble with the divorce problem is that, although the Church never forbade separation it has condemned divorce with the right to re-marry. Ideally speaking, this is no doubt right and is obviously in accord with the Christian ideal of one man—one wife. If the conditions of society make it almost impossible for this ideal to be implemented that is no reason for abolishing the ideal, but rather for improving social conditions.[1] Meanwhile, there are practical matters to be dealt with in a far more Christian spirit than is apparent to-day. Christian idealists may look forward, if they will, to a time when the abolition of divorce will be practicable, and will express the intention of Christ. But we must make society fit for such a step before it can be either tolerable or just.

Finally, a husband who has sex relationships with his wife, knowing a further pregnancy may endanger her life, or who does not see that adequate scientific precautions

[1] See Chapter IX.

are taken to prevent a pregnancy occurring, is acting in a most immoral manner and against all the laws of sexual behaviour.

4. Religious teaching which does not recognise physiological and psychological principles must be suspect.

Although our present knowledge of the nature of man is not final, the dogmatic assertions of traditional religion do not appear to square with Christ's moral principles. Are we not more concerned with bolstering up an already tottering moral edifice than with the reality of personal behaviour? Abortion and divorce, irregular sex unions and prostitution, perversions and delinquency, mental deficiencies and the propagation of the unfit, indicate the bankruptcy of our present system. The truth is that we do not possess a moral standard to-day; most of us make our own. That manufactured by society is so unreliable that we might as well disregard it. The laws governing marriage hamper the true expression of the highest that is in marriage, and should be altered to give the fullest possible expression to the principles of freedom and equality laid down by Christ. Our present moral code may appeal to the letter of the Gospels; but it is opposed to the spirit.

5. Sex is nothing to snigger about. Those who find it ludicrous do not understand its full meaning. They are usually obsessed with sex or frightened by it. They have not yet learned to fit it into their life pattern.

POSITIVE FACTORS

In endeavouring to construct positive principles, we must not be discouraged because, in the present state of society, some of them are impracticable. That cannot be helped; let us get the principles right first of all. Temporary compromise and social reorganisation can be considered later. We must have an ideal because without it we cannot muster our energies against those social conditions which militate against its achievement.

If the negative points just enumerated are correct, we

can say that personal relationships must be based on responsibility, respect for the personality of another individual, and sex-equality.

1. Personal relationships must be based on responsibility. This means that nothing may be done to harm another. But it is often difficult to decide what actually is harmful; therefore, we require understanding and knowledge. It is useless to ask people to act in a responsible manner if we do not provide them with adequate reasons for this behaviour. The first essential therefore is the *Acquisition of Knowledge*; of physical, psychological, sociological, and ethical facts. If it is true that Man is a social animal, it is equally true that he is a biological entity, and should be educated according to biological principles. But the acquisition of facts, of whatever order, is not in itself sufficient; they must be understood and interpreted correctly. Here lies our greatest difficulty. It is possible to give so many different interpretations: to be guided into so many different channels of thought, that it sometimes seems impossible to determine what is correct. We too often interpret facts as we wish, rather than in a dispassionate manner. Our life pattern will largely govern our interpretation. If it is positive, constructive, co-operative, and unselfish it will enable us to interpret our knowledge on a higher and more responsible plane than if it is negative, self-seeking and introspective.

2. The physical expression of the sex urge is only justifiable in active co-operation with a person of the opposite sex for mutual benefit. It is a dual relationship willingly entered into by free and understanding personalities.[1]

Individual sex expression, whether by actual physical stimulation or by mental fantasy, is a departure from the ideal and will not bring with it mental peace and harmony.

[1] There is a small minority of *true* homosexuals—and it is necessary to underline the word true, so as not to confuse them with the acquired type—to whom sexual experience with a person of the opposite sex would be as difficult and repugnant as homosexual experience to an ordinary heterosexual individual. A short discussion of this problem will be found in Chapter VIII.

Fc

3. The individual must go into action as a whole.

Just as the body is composed of millions of cells and various organs all carrying out their tasks independently— yet in closest co-operation—so must we correlate our different functions. The body cannot work without the mind nor the mind without the spirit. Our emotions, instincts, sentiments, and desires must be co-ordinated if the individual is to develop a full and balanced personality.

4. Sex energy is creative energy whether it is used in its biological sense, for reproductive purposes, or in wider realms, as of the arts. This is true both from a physiological and psychological point of view.

It has three main purposes:

    a. Reproduction.
    b. Mutual satisfaction.
    c. The development of the personality.

The highest expression of these aims is to be found in the present state of civilisation in a permanent monogamous union of two people of opposite sex, desirous of living together and bringing up a family.

4a. *Reproduction*

Most women do not complete their physiological life until they have had children. Neither does a man appreciate the full value of his own life until he has experienced the joys and responsibilities of parenthood. Children cement a marriage and make the group inter-dependent. It is essential that women should prove their fertility early, *but children should be wanted, definitely created, and properly spaced.* Illegitimate children should be unknown.

Those people who are likely to pass on mental or physical disease to children should, after due consideration, refrain from having children. This need not debar them from marriage providing the partner is made aware of the position. Indeed, many sub-normal people will lead better and more productive lives if they are happily married.

but they must practise an effective contraceptive technique
or be sterilized.[1]

4b. Mutual Appreciation

A woman may produce many children without appreciating the sex relationship in any way. It is equally
possible to enjoy the relationship physically without the
woman becoming pregnant. These two purposes of the
sex life are essential to a full and harmonious life. There
are times when they can and should be separated.

4c. Development of the Personality

It is only by the harmonious adjustment of the various
life forces that individuals will be enabled to act
reciprocally. Each must live unselfishly for the other. This
does not mean that they must be mutually self-sufficient;
but it does involve trust and mutual respect.

In an ideal sex relationship the physical must play a
prominent part. Thus a marriage devoid of the physical
is as one-sided as one based on the physical alone. In
discussing this problem the writers of the C.O.P.E.C.
report say: "The married relationship is at once physical
and spiritual, and can only come to its fullness if the couple
are one soul and one flesh. If the spiritual element is lacking,
bodily union becomes a degradation, if the bodily is lacking,
the spiritual can never reach its true completeness, and the
marriage remains on the level of an intimate friendship."[2]

5. Sex Experience must be unselfish.

We have had occasion to point out more than once the
duality of sex experience which is not always recognised.
Whilst it is perfectly true that the biological urge for
sex union is instinctive and egocentric, this is part of a
greater whole. Sex feeling is a composite mechanism
involving much more than mere physical desire. Its true
expression calls for men's highest qualities and it is because

[1] See p. 116.
[2] *The Relation of the Sexes*, p. 135. C.O.P.E.C. Commission Report.
Vol. IV.

this is not recognised more clearly that many sex unions fail entirely or are of the shortest duration.

6. Sex Experience has consequences.

Such an obvious remark seems scarcely worth making, yet even a superficial acquaintance with social behaviour shows that its implications are not appreciated by the vast majority. To many people "consequences" mean babies, and they think that if pregnancy is avoided all is well. But we have already seen that this is far from true. There are deep-seated psychological consequences which may have a permanent effect on the outlook and behaviour of one or both partners. How far these effects result from an injury of the individual's mind and personality and how far from economic and social restrictions which, if removed, would *ipso facto* remove the injury, is a debatable point. But the fact remains that as society is now constituted, the injury interferes with the harmonious functioning of the individual's mind. Emotions are let loose which need satisfaction and development in an atmosphere congenial to the make-up of that individual. Tensions and frustrations are created which frequently have unhappy consequences. If the waters of a river are allowed to flow over carefully prepared soil, growth and development will take place in the soil; crops and vegetation will appear for which further nourishment and care are required. Consequences have followed the original action. If the irrigation is stopped the crops will die and the development will cease. Similar consequences have followed the awakening of sex interests; the individual has embarked on a new series of experiences—that new development cannot be arrested without harm.

7. Sex Experience demands the union of two free and understanding personalities.

So far as they are able, both partners to the bargain must understand what is happening and what are the possible consequences. Physical union taking place as a result of a sudden attraction, or overwhelming emotional tension, is scarcely likely to stand the test of time, or to be experienced without eventual remorse or even recrimination. Such behaviour occurs at the instinctive level of our mental processes, and whilst it may be permissible for the biological species which have not progressed far along the evolutionary scale, it can hardly be considered adequate for one who is capable of thought and control. One of the highest developments of our mental processes lies in our capacity for "reflective thought". A more widespread exercise of this function would have most beneficial results on our sex lives. Indeed, not until a couple have passed through the sentimental stage of awe-struck adoration, and have reached that of reflection are they fit to consider themselves as free and understanding personalities, ready to embark on the sexual voyage.

Only three of the many criteria necessary to an ideal union will be discussed here.

In the first place, if both are free to choose, neither can be possessive. It is not intended to suggest that a couple cannot experience a sense of "oneness". The delightful experience of being signalled out from amongst a host of others as the one and only person to whom all may be given and from whom everything may be received, is wholly right. Such a feeling naturally involves some possessiveness, but of an unselfish kind. It is not just taking something. This possessiveness, whilst including a complete surrender, necessitates a complete giving, involving a desire to live and work for the other.

The possessiveness that is dangerous demands all and gives nothing; expects the other individual to subject every interest; to surrender work, friends, and social activities. The more people can learn to trust each other, and yet to permit and encourage the development of various interests, the greater will be their mutual respect and understanding.

A negative possessiveness leads to jealousy and lack of faith. The more possessive a man is in his attitude to women; the more unwilling he is to acknowledge feminine independence, the less certain is he of his sexual ability.

Possessiveness is the exact opposite of all that we mean by the equality of the sexes. It is particularly apparent in men and causes much unhappiness. It is one of the curses of modern sex life and is a relic of barbarism, when women were men's property.

Women are excluded by their constitution from certain conditions of labour, and well-fitted for others. The same may be said of men; each has his or her own contribution to make to the general well-being. If we could acknowledge these differences the world would be much happier. Sex differences will always exist but they must be respected and indeed expected.

This leads naturally to the second point—that women must not give all and receive nothing.

The third is equally important. If sex relationships are to be conducted with any semblance of equality, financial independence is essential. This does not mean that a man may not ever give money to a woman or pay for some joint expedition or amusement. But it means that a woman should be able to pay her way if she wishes, or at least contribute to the joint expenses. It is unfair on a man to feel that if he takes a girl out he must necessarily pay for both, or for a girl to feel, therefore, under an obligation to submit to some physical attention. There is no reason why a woman with plenty of money should not pay for an outing if the man is not so well off. Similarly, in marriage, an attempt should be made to provide the wife with money which she can spend without necessarily consulting her husband. A joint banking account may work, but it may be a terrible curse and a means of putting undue pressure on one partner. A woman should know something about the family income and have a say in the spending of it, particularly when the finances are run on a weekly budget system. In fact, each should know what money the other has, and have an opportunity of knowing how it is spent. Situations differ and each must be worked out on its merits, but according to the principles of equality and independence.

8. Sex union requires a knowledge of physical technique. This principle is by no means universally accepted; indeed the idea is entirely foreign to many people, particularly men, who often consider that they have nothing to learn, either because they have had some experience, or because they think that knowledge comes automatically to their sex. Many women encourage this attitude, although nothing could be further from the truth. Man possesses an instinct to mate, but it by no means follows that he knows how to exercise it. It requires practice and repetition for any instinct to be brought to perfection.

If a duckling is put into water it "instinctively" swims. "It used to be maintained that such instinctive behaviour was perfect from the beginning, but . . . more exact observation has shown that this is not strictly true, and that 'instinctive' behaviour only approaches perfection after considerable learning and experience, and therefore, even though the pattern may be established at birth, it is capable of considerable modification."[1]

An efficient love technique necessitates knowledge of matters such as the emotional differences between the sexes, anatomical and physiological constitution, the actual technique of coitus and the underlying principles of contraception. In addition, there must be complete mutual frankness and a willingness to exchange ideas and impressions.

The sooner men realise that the art of love is not learnt in a night, and cease to boast about their sexual prowess, the better. Similarly, the sooner women realise that they have a contribution to make to the relationship, and something to learn as well, the more chance will they have of experiencing real romance and lasting satisfaction. Patience and perseverance are essential to the fulfilment of any sex relationship, and therefore security, freedom from interruption, and some possibility of permanence are essential. Failure to achieve success can frequently be traced to lack of technique. The matter is of particular

[1] Gordon, Harris and Rees, *An Introduction to Psychological Medicine*, p. 38. Oxford Medical Publications.

importance when considering the whole problem of sex relationships, whether within or out of marriage. Technique is almost invariably left to take care of itself, or, at best, receives but the briefest consideration, although in fact it may take weeks, or even months, before a really satisfactory sex relationship is achieved. Preparation and education are therefore essential.

9. The motive behind the action must be "right", that is to say acceptable to the personality of both partners and to society. It must be directed towards the well-being of the individual, the family, and humanity in general.

10. Trust is an essential factor, which is impossible without complete frankness and understanding. It involves a capacity for forgiveness, since no one of us is perfect. The ups and downs of life must be tackled together. This is impossible without trust.

11. Other things being equal, there must be willingness to have children.

At present a variety of economic conditions are a bar to reproduction. Added to this is the fact that people require so many "luxuries" that children do not get a look in. Nevertheless, the intention should be to have children, provided, of course, the couple are fit to produce them.

Is it ever right to marry without the intention of having children? If there are medical or eugenic reasons against the production of children, that should be no bar to marriage. A husband and wife form a family even without children. There are a few people whose constitution is such that they neither want children nor are they fitted to have them. If they suspect this of themselves, and their suspicion is justified and not due to some hidden fear or even to laziness, it is probable that they would be well advised not to have children. They would probably prove inefficient parents. But there are women who say they do not want children because of some retardation of psychological growth; in such cases a child develops and improves the woman's whole personality. It is often necessary to obtain expert help to distinguish between these types.

Some writers go as far as to say that no marriage should be undertaken without the intention of having children, but in the light of modern scientific knowledge of the inheritance of disease this proposition is hardly tenable. Here again, the motive must be right.

In the main, however, we can say that if marriage is to last it must depend upon the functioning of the highest qualities of the personality in which the production of children will be one of the joys.

12. Our last and most important principle is this. There is no true union which does not accept a spiritual and physical content. What does this imply? It suggests that the only union which is really acceptable to God must include the full use and understanding of all our mental, physical, emotional and spiritual qualities. It presupposes the acceptance of all the principles we have already enumerated, not only in theory but in practice. It places marriage in the front line of Christian endeavour. One is tempted to ask whether Christian theologians have really accepted this statement with all its implications. They will agree about the spiritual, but are uncertain about the physical and emotional. One of the reasons for this hesitancy appears to be that celibacy and virginity have been over-emphasised in theological teaching for generations, and have come into direct opposition with the principles of marriage.

If some people have to accept the fact that marriage has a spiritual significance, which may bring the individual into a close relationship with God, others have to accept the fact that passion and emotional expression are the vital aspects of sex experience which, far from fogging spiritual insight and power, deepen and activate them. Both in marriage and celibacy we find a constant need for discipline, self-control and re-direction of energy. Both states are acceptable to God and both must lead ultimately to an understanding of God. If the theologians would accept these facts and encourage the ministers of religion to teach them we might get somewhere.

But, as we have already said, whilst accepting the theory they deny the practice or at best only encourage it in a half-hearted manner. The result is that many religious people feel that they are lowering their standards in some way if they permit themselves the experience of real emotional freedom in marriage. Many marriages would be far truer expressions of God's purpose if the couple not only accepted the theory but really translated it into practice. And so we reiterate that no union is acceptable to God which does not provide for the full use and development of those spiritual and physical qualities we have tried to enumerate. Every union therefore must be judged by this high standard. In so far as it is in accord with that standard, it is good; in so far as it falls short of this standard it is bad, both socially and spiritually.

It is scarcely necessary to add that being married does not automatically evoke any of these principles. Their observation, however, is essential to a creative union and such creative union is the most perfect experience of God's purpose for human nature.

CHAPTER VI

SEX RELATIONSHIPS AND SOCIETY

In so far as Beauty is a personal lust is it unfit for wholesome social ends. Only in so far as it is lifted above personal desire is it fitted to become a social inspiration.

HAVELOCK ELLIS, 1859-1939

WE HAVE BEEN somewhat academic. An endeavour has been made to unravel some of the tangled threads of moral behaviour; to understand the contribution that both Christianity and Science have to make to a more satisfactory sex ethic, and to formulate some principles upon which a new one should be based.

Now we are in a position to consider some practical points regarding sex relationships which arise naturally from the foregoing discussion. It is worth emphasising that people cannot be expected to conduct their sex lives with much hope of success unless they receive an adequate education in sex and subjects closely allied to it. Thus, by eighteen or twenty a boy or girl will have a really firm background of constructive knowledge with which to tackle the numerous problems that necessarily arise. Such instruction can be given in the home or school by parents or teachers, in college, university or club, by lectures and individual talks. Young people will then regard it as perfectly natural to seek help and advice when they are in difficulties or contemplating engagement or marriage.[1]

The first problem for consideration, because it is in the minds of most young people, and because of its widespread consequences, is that of sex relationships outside marriage.

SEX RELATIONSHIPS OUTSIDE MARRIAGE

We must distinguish between the different types of this relationship. We are not concerned with those unhappy affairs which are the result of brutal attack or mental deficiency, nor with those that are due to the ignorance or stupidity either of those who participate in the relationship or of their parents or guardians. Such behaviour would be impossible in an ideal society. Nor are we concerned, for the moment, with the sex relationship between an engaged couple, who, after clear thought, have decided to have some sex experience previous to marriage. This will be considered separately. Rather are we concerned with those young people who have a vague idea of marriage in the dim future, or who simply decide that they will have a sex experience because there is little chance of marriage and they are in "love" with each other and cannot see any particular reason against the procedure. We propose to

[1] See p. 194.

call this type of relationship an indiscriminate sex relationship.

INDISCRIMINATE SEX RELATIONSHIPS

We will start the discussion by asking whether "sexual freedom" leads to happiness or a more satisfying life?

In the light of what has been said it is fair to conclude that "sexual freedom" cannot lead to *permanent* happiness. It is true that a variety of affairs, or even one, may give temporary relief from an intolerable strain, and may provide individual satisfaction, but there is a great difference between satisfaction and happiness. The one is largely selfish; the other is akin to love and must therefore renounce the self. Let us consider this statement more closely. Many sex relationships are based on mere physical attraction. Though there may be every intention of making them last for some time they usually collapse at the end of a few months, because they lack so many of the essentials, and more especially as the physical experience on which they so largely depend is likely to prove unsatisfactory to one or both partners. And yet for this very reason many people would say that the relationship has served its purpose. Not only has it provided temporary happiness but it has proved to the satisfaction of the couple that they were unsuited to each other. Indeed, they may congratulate themselves on their sagacity, for, had they married, they would have created a hell for themselves from which escape would be difficult and expensive. But this is not sound reasoning. The satisfaction has, for the most part, been transitory and confined to one individual. Emotions have been unduly disturbed, and tensions created, and one or both are left with a sense of dissatisfaction and even resentment. Besides, the relationship has no resemblance to marriage. As a result they may try again with different partners or forswear sex. In the first case the result is hardly likely to be more satisfactory; in the second, definite psychological injury has been done which may bar the

way to successful marriage later on. Once sexual experience
has occurred many people feel that they have surrendered
something precious and may as well go on. Such reasoning
leads to disaster. Repeated sexual experience brings
instability of character, disinclination for a permanent
relationship, and excessive concentration on sexual affairs
which may eventually produce the type who is always
seeking sexual stimulation and self-gratification.

It is not true to say that a variety of sexual affairs trains
people to become expert lovers. It is arguable that a man
who has had one or two affairs before marriage may have
learnt some valuable lessons, and that a similar experience
for a woman may teach her how to avoid sexual pitfalls,
but in the majority of cases they may have acquired unsatisfactory habits or ideas which may spoil a future marriage
and, in any case, will be difficult to abolish. It is doubtful
if anything will have been acquired which cannot be learnt
by an intelligent couple who approach the marriage
relationship with thought and adequate preliminary
instruction.

Neither does it follow that a married man is necessarily
the best person to initiate a young girl. Many married
men are most unsatisfactory lovers and indeed are often
searching for another partner for this very reason.

Another point needs consideration. The principle of
equality is essential to a positive sex ethic. It follows from
this that if men are to have a variety of sex experiences
the same freedom must be allowed to women. Do women
need such freedom? Do they require sex experience as
much as men? We are now considering *people under thirty,
not married or older women.*[1] That being so, it seems probable
that the answer to both these questions is in the negative.
That young women are concerned with the problem is
obvious and natural, but it has not the same intense
significance that it has for many young men, although the
majority of women probably need sex experience at some

[1] The problem of married people and those over thirty will be
considered when we come to discuss extra-marital relationships.

time in their lives. The needs of *young* women, however, are different. To stir up their emotions and concentrate them in the sexual sphere has little to commend it. Once started the experience should be developed into a mature relationship involving security, home and children. The majority of women are not really satisfied with a sex relationship *per se ;* they require this wider background. Men, however, often appear quite satisfied with the physical side of the affair.

We must not, however, make the mistake of putting all women in the same category. Some are more emotionally mature than others and the need for sex experience is as strong as for many men. Nor for that matter are all men alike. We must pay more attention to these variations and not try and formulate a sexual ethic which tends to mould all people to the same pattern. Nevertheless, it is probably true to say that the majority of young women who embark on a series of sexual affairs are liable to do themselves considerable harm. The craving for excitement and new sensations may become an obsession from which it will be difficult to escape. They may fritter away their personalities until they reach a stage when they are incapable of experiencing strong affection for anyone.

The balance of psychological knowledge indicates that there are inborn psychological differences in the requirements of the sexes which will not be settled by permitting *unlimited* sexual freedom to either sex.

Of one thing we can be certain. To embark on any course of action which is intended to separate sexual energy from the whole personality is to cause disruption and tension. It is tantamount to saying that sexual energy is greater and more powerful than the whole personality —that the individual is subject to his or her sexual energy instead of the sexual energy being under the control of the personality.

The foregoing discussion has reduced itself to a consideration of physical behaviour. This is inevitable because the majority of these relationships are concerned mainly with physical matters. The initial attraction is largely physical and the expression given to the relationship is equally so. And yet we have seen that the true appreciation of sex cannot be experienced on the physical plane alone. Here lies the danger of all such one-sided and immature relationships. Their advocates harp always on their essential value in helping people to decide whether or not they are really suited to marry, but in truth marriage and the type of relationship we are discussing are quite different experiences impossible to compare because the same fundamental factors are not present.

In an indiscriminate relationship the couple meet only under exceptional circumstances, and when both are more or less keyed up for physical union. Very often they see each other only when on their best behaviour. A dinner or dance once or twice a week followed by a stolen night is in no way similar to the every-day experience of marriage. Even a holiday of some duration cannot be compared with the ordinary marriage relationship. The couple are still only seeing each other under the best conditions. Each partner usually has his or her own occupation which is conducted under other conditions and does not obtrude itself. Petty worries are kept in the background; the physical dominates the situation. Even that is surrounded by an artificial glamour. When that fades, and carelessness creeps in, the relationship dies because it possesses none of the essentials of permanence and stability. It is largely because the physical is unsatisfactory that the affair comes to an end. Because they are so much in love with each other, and because the desire for coitus is so strong, young people imagine the physical will work automatically. Nothing could be farther from the truth. If the technique is wrong the relationship will probably break down. This applies to all sex relationships.

Technique cannot be acquired in a few hours. It requires time, patience and understanding. We have already seen that men seem to think that because a certain degree of physical satisfaction comes easily to them, this knowledge is sufficient for them really to satisfy women, whilst women imagine that they have only to leave matters to the man for everything to be all right. Both are frequently disillusioned. This aspect of the problem is stressed because it is not yet sufficiently appreciated. In addition, if an extraneous fear, such as the possibility of discovery or the pricking of an uneasy conscience, or even the need for haste, should obtrude itself, that alone is sufficient to prevent the woman from giving herself wholly and fully in body and mind and thus experiencing a proper orgasm. In such cases women "hold themselves back" and eventually become cold or frigid. In addition, since the nature of the relationship would make pregnancy a calamity, contraceptive technique must be equally satisfactory. Here again little care is taken, reliance often being put on contraceptives that are useless, aesthetically objectionable or otherwise unsuitable.

No sex relationship is going to be satisfactory unless all these matters are carefully thought out and provided for—unless the "setting" is right. If the relationship is hurried or furtive—the individuals feel besmirched. It must be obvious, therefore, that the majority of these ill-conceived, hurriedly performed relationships are doomed to failure from their inception. The whole affair seems to be so natural—so fatally easy—that the pitfalls are not appreciated until too late. If it breaks down, that is often an incentive to try again in order to prove that it was the partner and not the relationship that was at fault. Those who indulge in these affairs will not be found to be happier or more contented than those who do not. On the contrary, there is a noticeable restlessness and craving for emotional excitement which is out of all proportion to the natural requirements of the individual.

Marriage, on the other hand, is, or should be, based on something quite different. It is not a partnership that can be altered or broken at will, but rather the development of a new and permanent relationship between two people. It is the starting point of a life-long adventure and embodies real love, mutual respect, responsibility, permanence and security. The couple should be good friends, learning to work and play together as well as to make love. Success in marriage depends ultimately on spiritual insight and power. It requires the capacity for unselfish devotion and a willingness to face the ups and downs of life cheerfully and with understanding. Most of these factors are necessarily absent from an indiscriminate relationship. It would clear the air considerably if people could recognise these differences and cease trying to compare the two.

The type of sex relationship for men that seems to be accepted as sufficient by the general body of society, seems to consist of a little preliminary love-making—often at the end of a long day—quickly followed by coitus which does not last long. There is little attempt to ensure that the woman is really satisfied or to discuss mutual feelings. This lack of constructive mutual conversation is most noticeable. Little attention is paid to the "setting". For women the same general idea prevails. If they are honest they will say that they had hoped for something better—something more lasting, but that "it can't be helped"; that they have not sufficient time in which to obtain any orgasm and are frequently left in a highly emotional state. Such a situation is common amongst all sections of the community. The fault is not always due to the man. Some women are non-co-operative. They think it is their duty to be loved; but not to love actively. They do not face up to the realities of sexual intercourse and are equally disinclined to exhibit or experience a real freeing of emotional feeling. Intercourse quickly becomes unsatisfactory and even repugnant to them and they blame their husbands for faults which really lie in themselves.

Gc

FRIGIDITY

It is from such unsatisfactory relationships that the frigid woman is bred. Frigidity shows itself in many different ways and has, of course, many different causes, some of which must be dated back to bad parental influence in early years. Nevertheless, there is little doubt that much frigidity is due to the fact that the woman is never properly awakened; there is no free flow of emotional life. She is willing to be awakened but it just does not happen. Very often the man has so many inhibitions; his own emotions are so restrained and taut that it is impossible for him ever really to awaken his wife. She never gets a chance and soon develops inhibitions of her own which merely make matters worse and create a vicious circle that is difficult to break.

Many men perform the sex act more or less mechanically. Such orgasm as they have is of very little permanent value. The physical desire is there but is only accepted on the biological plane. There is no freeing of the whole personality, no acceptance of the beneficial aspects of sex; no acceptance of passion as a true expression of personality. Indeed, passion to them is unknown because they regard it as giving way to the baser instincts and so it is not quite nice—it is not really "done", except of course with women of low moral character. There are thousands of men like that all over the country. They make moderately satisfactory husbands and produce excellent children and in fact are quite proud of themselves. There is an active repression working in them all the time making them self-contained, jealous, spiteful and sadistic, or alternatively so "spiritually" minded that any outward emotional expression would be too painful to contemplate. They are amazed when their wives run off with someone else. Had they been taught a little before marriage much of this might have been avoided.

Orgasms vary in intensity. Some, in which there is a

complete freeing of the whole personality, are highly
beneficial; others, in which the relief is purely physical,
are of little permanent value. Being so unsatisfactory there
is an instinctive feeling of frustration and a desire to
repeat the act quickly so as to make a better job of it.
Such men are often considered to be "highly sexed" by
their wives. In reality they are sexually starved. They
have never experienced real emotional relief and have
never let themselves go in all parts of their being. Thus
tension is created and they often do themselves harm.
Their emotions are boxed up. They are like a jack-in-the-
box who has only managed to get out a couple of arms
from under the lid. Until they undo the string and jump
right out of the box they will remain on a low level of
emotional development. Such men create frigid women.
If the situation is recognised it can frequently be cured.
If it is not, trouble will arise which, as we have said, may
end in the woman running away with someone else. If
she does, she is legally in the wrong and is socially condemned. But the fault is not hers. Neither is it really his.
Rather is it the parental and social upbringing to which
each has been subjected and the ridiculous stupidity
which allows them to get married without giving them any
teaching. If it is impossible to put matters right, they
should be separated. Should they take new partners
some provision should be made to ensure that the same
situation does not arise in the new relationship.

There are, of course, many other causes of frigidity
in women, and the manner in which this frigidity shows
itself varies enormously. There is the woman whose whole
life is centred in her household duties; the woman always
striving after new effects or embarking on new love affairs,
always trying to find the man who will satisfy her. Or
there is the resigned wife and the frivolous wife and the
grumbling wife, who is always humiliating her husband
in public. Whatever else these women are suffering from
they all have one thing in common—some degree of
frigidity. Many of their troubles could have been avoided

had they had pre-marital instruction, or had the matter been investigated soon after marriage, when they found that things were not quite right. To acquiesce in such unsatisfactory relationships for months and years is truly lamentable.

To describe the ideal relationship is beyond the scope of this book. Suffice it to say that sex relationships must be prepared for carefully; must never be hurried or disturbed; must be mutually desired and technically correct and of sufficient length to provide a mutual orgasm.[1] A clitoral "sensation" is not the same as a real orgasm which includes the whole being.

We see, therefore, that there is little to be said for indiscriminate relationships. They exist almost entirely because our social structure is so arranged that there is no alternative for the majority of healthy young people.

YOUTHFUL MARRIAGES

The main criticism of youthful marriages and of the so-called war marriages is not that they take place but that they are so badly prepared for. There is little difference between some of these marriages and indiscriminate relationships; they are doomed to failure from the start. It is sad that they should be tolerated in an enlightened society, especially when their evil effects could be minimised by adequate preparation. Is it reasonable to suggest that young people should remain continent until they are nearly thirty or that women should be debarred from sex experience until they are about twenty-five?

It is not suggested that it is impossible for young people to remain continent or that continence is harmful. It is perfectly possible and not at all harmful provided the condition is not too prolonged and there is a definite ideal in view, and provided further that the emotions are not roused prematurely, either by a violent affair or by

[1] See *Sex Factor in Marriage*, Helena Wright. *Modern Marriage and Birth Control*, Edward F. Griffith. *Ideal Marriage*, Van de Velde.

environmental conditions. A prolonged and enforced continence breeds a host of ills that militate against satisfactory marital relations later on. But society does everything in its power to stir up the emotions by such means as slums, poverty, over-crowding, cinemas and drinks; added to which it supplies no educational background and no satisfactory principles of sexual knowledge on to which young people can hold. It demands a high standard without providing the means to achieve it, and it insists upon a segregated education for a large section of our youthful population until about eighteen, and then throws the sexes together in university, college or factory, expecting them to conduct themselves decorously and decently. It speaks well for the innate common sense of youth that they manage as well as they do. At a slightly later age it forbids marriage, saying that they are too young to know their own minds. In addition, parents keep a tight hold on the money bags and expect the young folk to put up with long engagements instead of encouraging them to marry, and providing facilities until such time as they can afford to stand on their own feet.

Neither is it suggested that all people should automatically marry young; they may not be sufficiently mature. But there seems no real reason why a couple should not marry and continue with their studies; why they should not live and work together, or continue with their respective occupations for a time. One finds the same kind of difficulty in all social groups. Bank clerks, policemen, soldiers, young men in the professions, teachers and many others are discouraged or actually prevented from marrying for many years; some indeed lose their jobs if they marry. The bachelor is paid as much as the married man; the family man receives the same wage as the married man with no children. Girls work in the factories because their labour is cheaper than that of their young men who, in all probability, have no work at all. Nor have the girls time to make themselves proficient at household duties.

In fact, the only people for whom marriage is an advantage are the unemployed; it is cheaper for two people to live in one room and far warmer. As Mr. Orwell tells us: "A working-class bachelor is a rarity, and so long as a man is married, unemployment makes comparatively little alteration in his way of life." [1]

It is not surprising that families are small and men hesitant to embark on the responsibilities of marriage. This hesitation has contributed largely to the problem of indiscriminate relationships, because many girls find that the only way in which they can obtain male companionship is by permitting sex union. If they will not agree to this they find that they are thrown over for other girls who are less particular. Such behaviour is contrary to the natural desire of most young people.

As far as practical considerations are concerned, young people should aim at marriage rather than at anything less. If an engaged couple find they will have to wait for years until marriage becomes a possibility, they might well consider a secret marriage. There are many young women working in jobs from which they would be dismissed were it known that they were married. The result is that their engagements are unduly prolonged because the man simply cannot earn enough to support them both. This is utterly unfair and thoroughly antisocial. Were they married and both working they would probably be able to keep a little home going. They would at least have their evenings, and would not have the strain of a long engagement to add to their other difficulties. It is perfectly possible to find small flats within the means of such a couple. Let them then seriously consider marrying secretly, without the knowledge of their respective employers. These outrageous conditions of employment demanded by many short-sighted government departments and private companies can most effectually be broken down if they are generally disregarded. Of course, the young couple would be well advised to take into their

[1] *The Road to Wigan Pier*, p. 81.

confidence their parents and close friends. Such a procedure has its disadvantages, but they are not so great as the strain of a long engagement or the uncertainty and insecurity of a pre-marital relationship. The fact that the couple were really married would tend to unite them in a way that a pre-marital relationship would never achieve. They would have their ups and downs but they would have the pleasure and joy of working them out together. Many such marriages exist and work very well. Here again, however, we must stress the fact that the couple should obtain proper help and preparation.

One often finds people saying that the responsibilities of marriage are too great, by which they really mean that they have not the courage to take the plunge. There is a great deal of selfishness about marriage to-day; the mountains are so big that they appear to be unclimbable. But marriage is never easy. Nor for that matter is life easy although it is frequently made easier by a happy marriage in which there is intention and purpose. We might well take a leaf out of our grandparents' book of life and adopt their philosophy. This is what the great surgeon Sir James Paget had to say about marriage after experiencing it for nearly forty years: "In May, 1844, I married and began to enjoy that happiness of domestic life which has already lasted without a break, without a cloud, for 39 years. From this time the 'being alone' was the being alone with one who never failed to love, in wise counsel, in prudence, and in gentle care of me. With her it was easy to work and be undisturbed by anything going on around me; a habit which I can advise everyone to learn. Her admirable music and her singing, with a matchless gentle voice, and a pure, culti- vated style, were a refreshing accompaniment to my evening reading and writing, and when these were over she wrote for me, copying for the press my roughly written manuscripts, sitting with me till midnight or far into the morning, all alone, or, after a time, with the baby brought down in its cradle and watched and fed.

"I can recommend the plan to all young married people. It is an intensely happy one and may teach them to work in the midst of what are commonly called interruptions. I owe to it that I have never once needed to leave my family or any tolerably quiet party of friends in order to work alone or undisturbed; whether for writing, reading or any similar work, no kind of good music or talking has ever interrupted me. I have thoroughly enjoyed them even while at work." [1]

To sum up, therefore, we may say:

1. That the more closely a sex relationship approximates to the basic principles laid down in the last chapter, the greater is the chance of success and permanence. These principles are the same for all men and women and apply to *all* sex relationships.

2. That in so far as indiscriminate relationships occur under conditions opposed to all that a perfect sex relationship should be, they are a failure.

3. That the present unsatisfactory state of affairs is due to society's failure to formulate a sex ethic which will improve social morality and encourage marriage and parenthood.

4. That it is unfair to expect young people to remain sexually continent for ten to fifteen years in our present state of civilisation.

5. That the majority of sexual deficiencies, broken marriages and anti-social behaviour have their roots in unsatisfactory sexual habits and ideas acquired before marriage.

6. That the cure for these conditions lies in a fundamental change of outlook regarding the place of sex education in the life of the community and in early marriage, preceded by adequate instruction.

7. That, for the most part, indiscriminate relationship, and marriage are so essentially dissimilar that they cannot be compared.

[1] *Memories and Letters*, ed. Stephen Paget, p. 128. Longmans, Green & Co., 1901.

8. That it is advisable for anyone contemplating a sex union of any kind whatever to obtain expert medical advice and help. The assistance which can be given at this time by an understanding physician, both practically, and by dispassionate discussion, is invaluable.

We may answer the question we originally asked by saying that there is no evidence that sexual freedom leads to greater happiness or a more satisfactory life.

PRE-MARITAL RELATIONSHIPS

We have by no means exhausted the subject yet. Some engaged couples ante-date their marriage physically. They have probably thought the matter out most carefully and have concluded that it would be unwise to tie themselves permanently without making quite certain that the physical is as satisfactory as they hope it will be. Their argument proceeds along the following lines. It is well-known that the majority of unhappy marriages fail on the physical sphere, often as a result of mismanagement in the early stages. It by no means follows because a couple are satisfactory lovers that they are equally satisfactory bed-fellows; they may even find themselves antagonistic when it comes to the most intimate relationship. It would therefore be wise to put the matter to the proof. As the argument against this type of relationship is that it is impossible to bring about a situation in any way comparable to that of marriage itself, we will make our experiment as similar to marriage as possible. We will take our parents and friends into our confidence; we will go away together quite openly; we will arrange our lives so that we see each other in all possible moods and phases, in getting up, having a head-ache, and contending with a difficult situation. We will, of course, practise an efficient contraceptive technique, and seek medical help and advice before doing anything at all. The arrangement will be continued for as long as we consider it necessary to come to a definite decision. When we have made up our minds we will marry or separate. If we do marry we shall at least know that we have more than a theoretical chance of making a success of the job. If we separate there will be no recriminations.

The above is a fair statement of a position taken up by many intelligent people to-day. There are several important points: motives and actions are carefully thought out and definitely idealistic. There is nothing hidden about the relationship which is a family affair dependent on the active co-operation and understanding of the respective parents. The arrangements are such that the couple see each other under good and bad conditions. No children are to be born, so that effective contraception is essential.

That such relationships are on the increase is well recognised; that they are possible is due to the effectiveness of contraception. That they are on quite a different footing from those we have discussed previously is equally obvious; they embody the majority of the principles we have considered and do not exclude the possibility of future children; indeed they visualise marriage and children as the rightful and proper outcome of the relationship. They are often successful and end in happy balanced marriages; indeed, many of them only differ from marriage in the fact that there is no preliminary ceremony, either civil or religious. Those who believe in this type of relationship argue that the ceremony which follows eventually is entered into with a greater sense of responsibility, and is more likely to be really binding than one in which the physical is an unknown quantity or has already resulted in an unsatisfactory sex union and the unintended creation of a child.

These ideas are new and will have to be considered seriously by society as a constructive attempt to stabilise marriage in its truest sense. The following questions are relevant:

1. Supposing the relationship is not found to stand the test of time, and proves unsatisfactory from the physical

point of view, and is therefore broken off, will the effect on the individuals be worse than if they had married and found out their mistake afterwards?

2. Would an extension of such a system serve to strengthen the marriage unit in society and diminish the incidence of divorce, or would the reverse be the case? Would the principle of monogamous union be strengthened or weakened?

3. There is here a definite separation of the sex needs of individuals from their reproductive needs. The former is visualised in a more personal context, the latter in a more social one. Is there any reason why these needs should not be considered and legislated for separately, provided the final intention is to have home and children?

4. Have we not tended in the past to put too much emphasis on the sexual act as such and not enough emphasis on its consequences? How would such a system affect our attitude to this question?

5. If two people went to a parson and explained the conditions under which they had been living and the reasons for this course of action and asked to be married in church, would he marry them or not? If not, why not? Have they sinned and fallen from a state of grace?

6. If two people who had an indiscriminate relationship which resulted in a pregnancy, went to the parson with a similar request, would he marry them? If so, why?

Is the answer to both these questions that, from a Christian point of view, both partners have sinned to some extent and so both must admit their sin and receive forgiveness before they can marry? Or is the answer more a question of procedure than of sin or moral lapse; that the rules of the Church forbid a priest marrying a couple who have already had sex union, unless the couple have admitted their fault? But can we compare the two conditions; the one planned and considered from all angles; the other haphazard and thoughtless? In the first case

it may be admitted that the couple have acted contrary
to the present rules of society and of the Church, but
we cannot help wondering whether they have committed a
sin against God's will. Their whole motive has been
towards marriage. In the second case the couple have
not only offended social and religious laws but they
have certainly acted contrary to God's will and have
in some measure sinned. Even here we must ask what
proportion of sin rests on the couple and what proportion
rests on society for allowing them to be so ignorantly
brought up.

The point we wish to make is that neither the Church
nor society distinguishes between the two conditions;
both have offended against the law, therefore both most
be punished. It is true that the punishment is not very
severe; society is becoming more and more tolerant of
these lapses and most couples are married quietly in
church. Nevertheless, a stigma remains; an offence has
been committed. But this is most unfair because the two
situations are really quite different and yet they are treated
with the same degree of disapproval. Must we not conclude
that there is something wrong with the social and religious
rules? Should they not be redrawn? Is there any evidence
that Christ condemned a sex union previous to marriage
where the couple had thought the matter out and stated
publicly and before witnesses their intention to marry?
Is there any evidence that society accepted this situation;
that "betrothal" permitted sex union?

Why should not the Church institute and accept "betrothal", by which we mean a public ceremony for which
there had been previous instruction and in which the
couple stated their intention of marrying in the future,
provided they found they were fully suited to each other?
In fact, it would be a type of novitiate before the final
marriage vows were taken. And there would have to be
no children and a time limit. This matter is of considerable importance and is considered in greater detail on
page 153.

In order to clarify our thinking we have considered sex relationships outside marriage under various easily distinguishable categories, which really indicate different stages of emotional development. The maintenance of the family unit being the basis of our social structure, the perfectly adjusted marriage must be our ideal. The pre-marital relationship is a stage in its development. Indiscriminate relationships are anti-social and have no place in a properly ordered society. Nevertheless, it is doubtful if they will ever disappear entirely. There is, however, yet one more category to be considered before we can consider the difficult problem of extra-marital relationships.

TEMPORARY RELATIONSHIPS

Many young people feel that whilst they do not wish to marry at present they do wish to express in a physical manner the real affection they feel for each other. This affection is based on a genuine feeling of comradeship and differs from both indiscriminate and pre-marital relationships. The couple do not visualise marriage and so they rule out children and use contraceptives. Their attitude to the sex act differs entirely from that of the older generation. To them it has no special significance. They do not feel that they can do everything else bar that one thing. It appears to be a perfectly natural and indeed desirable result of their love. They do not say all this in so many words but this is a fair description of their attitude. And what is still more interesting is that they do not show any of the feelings of guilt or shame that have dogged the steps of their elder brothers and sisters. For this reason, one cannot say that the relationship is likely to prove so emotionally unsatisfactory. The whole thing appears to be perfectly natural. There are many who will condemn this attitude outright, but that will not alter the fact that the situation exists. Nor indeed is it desirable that we should adopt this attitude. There is far more in the situation than that. These young people view life differently and they react differently. Their attitude to life is essentially healthy and positive. Their emotional reactions are, on the whole, much. healthier. They do not rule out marriage. On the contrary, they believe in it and look forward to it—in the future. But they are not necessarily going to marry the first person they have a sex relationship with.

What are we to say about this type of relationship? It is an entirely different relationship to the others. It is not on the same level as an indiscriminate relationship, neither is it a pre-marital relationship—nor of course is it marriage. Many of our principles, however, are fulfilled. The affair is planned and thought out. It is mutually desired and is recognised for what it is—a temporary relationship. There is no particular attempt at secrecy as most of the couple's friends know what is happening and indeed are probably doing the same thing themselves. There are no guilty feelings. If there were the whole situation would be open to immediate criticism. If it is objected that the reproductive aspect is ignored, it might be argued with equal force that many marriages, which accept the reproductive aspect, ignore emotional harmony. Neither can it be said that the motive for the use of contraceptives is altogether wrong. The couple are drawing a still greater distinction between the two main purposes of the sex relationship. There is a more distinct separation between the reproductive purpose and the emotional needs of the individual. But there is no denial of the ultimate value of the family and children—merely a postponement.

That it is an immature relationship seems clear. It would, however, be wrong to condemn the relationship because it is not ideal. We do not live in an ideal world and we do not provide ideal conditions for our young people to grow up in. It is probable that with more effective education and more opportunities for early planned marriages the need for this type of relationship would diminish. It may be that it is a product of the emotional stresses and severe economical conditions under which we are now living. People are different; their needs are different and their reactions are different. Whilst doing our best to create the ideal situation in which the majority of people make planned and happy marriages, we must recognise these differences more honestly than we have done in the past.

In discussing this problem in his book, *Sex Morality To-morrow*, Kenneth Ingram points out that there are various degrees of love. Our future society will have to be willing to accept these variations and be more tolerant. Beyond this, it is impossible to go at present. The situation is changing too quickly. Of one thing we may be certain. If we are fighting for individual liberty, we must accept the' implications which go with that state. If we do not like the situation, if this type of relationship, for instance, in the light of further evidence, appears to be productive of anti-social traits, we must pay more attention to our education· programme and less to the policy of laissez-faire.

EXTRA-MARITAL RELATIONSHIPS

These affairs are most complicated and difficult. As one of the partners is already married they strike a deep blow at family stability and individual harmony. They create deep emotional disturbances and often arouse feelings of jealousy and hatred. They are far below the ideal we have set before us and yet they are very common. Amongst many causes three may be mentioned.

In the first place, the original marriage having failed in some way one, at least, of the partners is full of discontent. Secondly, many young women like older men. They find them more satisfactory to talk to, more knowledgeable and more sure of themselves. And very often, having more money, they can do things in a better style. In fact, they are more "interesting". But alas! They are already married! In the third place there are more women than men in the country and so there are not enough men to go round. As a matter of fact the discrepancy between the sexes is not so great as is often suggested, although it is sufficiently serious to have an effect on our problem. According to the Statistical Review for England and Wales for 1937 (Table 1, part 1) there were then 19,705,000 males and 21,326,000 females, a difference of a little over one and a half million extra females. From 0–5 years there were more males than females. At fifteen the sexes were practically equal. From twenty to thirty there were roughly 100,000 more females than males in each five-year group. At forty there were roughly 245,000 more females than males whilst at eighty-five there were twice as many—73,760 females to only 35,900 males!

The important age group from our point of view is the twenty to thirty group. Even allowing for all those women who are not particularly anxious to marry or are unfit to marry for some reason or other, there still remains a large discrepancy. Most women probably hope to marry before they are about thirty and feel their chances decreasing after they have passed that age, although many do, of course, marry and start families well on into the thirties. Nevertheless, there is a great temptation for these older women to embark on an extra-marital relationship. Many such women have their own jobs and interests and their sex needs, which are often acute, differ slightly from those of younger women whose minds are set more on home and children. The older ones have probably resigned themselves to the fact that homes and children are not for them, indeed, they may not want them. But they often feel the need for sex experience if only to "work it out of their system" as one woman expressed it to the writer.

Beyond drawing attention to the fact that this problem exists it is not our intention to consider it here. It is one of extreme difficulty and great individuality in which much sympathy and understanding are essential, if any constructive help is to be given. The most important practical advice that one can give is to urge women who find themselves in real difficulty over the matter to seek help and guidance and not bottle up their emotions and feelings for years. There are plenty of doctors and parsons about who are well qualified to help. The value of talking out the problem with another person is most beneficial in itself. And yet how many people have the courage to take the plunge?

What courses are open to a couple who find that their marriage is in danger of going wrong? Occasionally one partner realises what is happening before the other. In this case the situation should be faced and the other partner told. What so often happens is that an outside person is told and the partner is left guessing. This is not right. If only the couple would face up to the problem together they might solve it for themselves or agree to get expert help. The criticism is frequently made that outsiders cannot help. This is inaccurate as the following example will show.

A delightful young couple—both under thirty—had been married for four years and had two young children. Eighteen months ago—just after the birth of the second child, the wife left the husband because she found that he had been "carrying on" with another woman. The husband admitted this but said it was merely a temporary lapse owing to the fact that his wife did not make him happy sexually. After a few months the couple came together again for the sake of the children and because they were genuinely fond of each other. However, the wife did not trust her husband and was always asking him where he had been, why he was late and with whom he had been out. He maintained that the affair was finished; that he was genuinely desirous of making the marriage a success, but that his wife still did not make him happy and was not trusting him. To this she replied that she saw little value in sex, that he should control himself, and that they already had enough children. Of course, she watched her husband; who wouldn't? Four things were pointed out

Hc

to her. Firstly, that there was another aspect of marriage than the reproductive. Secondly, that her knowledge of contraception and technique was practically nil. Thirdly, that marriage must be based on trust. Fourthly, the emotional needs and differences between the sexes was explained to her. As a result of all this re-education which of course included the learning of an effective contraceptive method, the attitude of the couple completely changed and the original harmony returned in a stronger and more mature form. The wife ceased to watch her husband, enjoyed her sex relationship and looked a different person, whilst the husband ceased to say that his wife was cold and did not make him happy. It may be presumed that the marriage was saved, but it would have been dissolved had they not sought help. There are hundreds of similar cases throughout the whole country that could be easily put right, but often drift into separation and divorce.

If a divorce appears inadvisable for some reason or other, separation may be tried. This is a most unsatisfactory situation and almost always leads to the formation of one or more irregular unions, which are of little value to the people concerned, and rarely last any length of time. A separation is often forced on people—women in particular—by the hateful possessiveness of the other partner who, by refusing to acknowledge his own failure, derives a certain amount of pleasure by taking it out on the woman, thereby bolstering up the tottering edifice of his own self-esteem. Still more unfortunately the law often supports him and provides him with weapons he does not deserve—the custody of the child, for instance, which usually becomes his if he finds his wife has eventually committed adultery and he cares to start divorce proceedings. And yet the child is often the one thing that the woman wants and is really justified in keeping.

Finally, the couple may decide to stay together—largely on account of the children—but agree that each may go his own way.

The chief of a variety of objections to this arrangement is that whilst one partner may be satisfied with it, it by no means follows that the other is equally content. More often than not the man can accommodate himself whilst the woman is left in an unhappy dilemma. Her main interests are in her home and children, and she may find it very difficult to discover a lover who, whilst satisfying her physical needs, is willing to play second fiddle to the husband. In all probability she has to decide between her feelings and her children and an undesirable state of emotional tension is set up whichever wins. Here again, it is impossible to discuss these problems in detail. They are far too varied and individual and are outside the scope of this book. Nevertheless, they are terribly important and need solution.[1] The worst possible thing to do is to pretend the situation does not exist or fail to face up to it. So often does one find that selfishness and jealousy and obstinacy are at the root of the trouble. So often is it necessary to be honest and unselfish and tolerant and forgiving. Far too many couples rush to the lawyer before making any real attempt to settle their differences. What many need, of course, is a change of heart; a change in their philosophy of life. A truly difficult task.

All these situations are wrong and far below our ideal because all the individuals are out of harmony in a greater or less degree. There is tension and strain instead of peace and happiness and mutual confidence. As long as the personality is outraged in this manner so long will the individual life be unsatisfactory. Decision when it comes will only be right if spiritual values are recognised and accepted. The thought must be directed towards the welfare of the other. Any action or mode of behaviour in which the elements of progress are prohibited or restrained from their natural development is not ideal and some degree of wrongness or sin has entered in. There are, how-

[1] Two books that are particularly helpful to women are: *The Way of All Women*, Esther Harding. Longman Green & Co. 1934; *The Single Woman*, Laura Hutton. Balliere Tindall & Cox.

ever, definite degrees of wrongness. The man who refuses to release his wife when all love has gone is, in the writer's opinion, committing a sin. Or take the case of the man-mistress relationship. At one end of the scale we find the man who uses the woman entirely for his own ends and discards her when he has finished with her, whilst at the other end is the type of relationship in which the thought of each is toward the benefit of the other. The man encourages emotional and psychological development in the woman and does not seek to possess her body and soul. He will not be surprised, therefore, if he finds her falling in love with someone else and wishing to marry and have children. It may be hard for him because he feels a deep affection for her although he cannot marry her. Nevertheless, his love has brought about this situation and he must willingly accept and even encourage it.

No! One cannot always assess the degree of wrongness.

It can, of course, be argued that all these situations are wrong, and that marriage vows having been accepted are life-long. We have already agreed that this is the ideal, but we have indicated some of the weaknesses of this position. Many other situations having failed to reach the ideal are wrong. Nevertheless, whilst maintaining our ideal and working for its achievement have we not to make the best of two evils? When things have gone wrong, is it not the duty of Christian people to recognise that there is no longer any course open which is free from all objection ; some losses have to be cut? Should they not be cut in a manner most likely to produce future balance and harmony? Must we not give all the help that we can to the best of our ability? That is the writer's opinion. Thus, whilst acknowledging that these situations are fraught with peril, it appears wiser to make the best readjustments that are possible in the light of modern knowledge and understanding. And let us add that as the question involves serious problems of conscience the individual should seek spiritual help and guidance as well as material help from the doctor. Incidentally, there is room here for a much closer co-operation between the doctor and parson.

In seeking advice, the couple have to face the fact that they may come to realise that the proposed course of action is not the right solution.

One further point. If these situations are so far from the ideal, has not the individual to consider whether he must not work out the problem for himself without involving another personality, which may be hurt, however carefully he conducts the affair? Will he not find a greater sense of power in sacrificing part of himself for this greater benefit and development that can be obtained through a strict dicipline? This is a matter which can only be settled by the individual himself, but it is an aspect of the whole affair which must not be neglected.[1]

Finally, as we have already seen, sex experience is not essential to women any more than it is to men. There are plenty of other activities into which sex energy can be creatively transferred. Nevertheless, the road will be difficult and a quiet mind will not be achieved without a struggle, and the acceptance of the condition by the whole personality. One cannot just sublimate one's sex emotions by an act of will because sublimation is really an unconscious process.

PROSTITUTION

We have avoided a discussion of prostitution because it is anti-social and thoroughly bad. It is quite outside the conception of sexual behaviour we are considering. Nevertheless, we may consider whether temporary relationships are of more spiritual value than prostitution. All pre-marital relationships in the sense in which the term is used here, and many indiscriminate relationships, are based upon an entirely different conception of sexual behaviour than that possible with prostitution. However misguided a couple

[1] See p. 133 for an elaboration of this point.

may be, however far they may have strayed from the ideal, there is little doubt that the germ of something finer is to be found in the relationship. In prostitution there is merely a financial transaction accompanied by a biological relief of tension, with little or no consideration for the personality or feelings of the woman.

CHAPTER VII

MARRIAGE, PARENTS AND CHILDREN

> Parents are as it were the masters of their children's countenances, because the face depends upon the sentiments of the mind, the sentiments upon the education and the education upon the parents. If the child's features are not regular, the parents cannot give them a just regularity. But it lies in their power to form the mind and the heart of the child, and it is by forming of these that they are able to mould the air of his face.
>
> ORTHOPAEDIA. 1743

EVERY COUNTRY OR group of people has always had its social laws to which the individuals were expected to conform. Those laws were made for the good of the whole community, though this does not say that they were always the best that could be attained. There is little doubt that many of those that regulate our present social conduct are unacceptable to a large proportion of the population, being based on traditions and ideas which are outworn and irksome. Nevertheless, whilst they exist we must conform to them, although we may agitate for their alteration. It is only by the creation of an enlightened public opinion that the laws will eventually be amended. A typical example of this can be seen in the present agitation for the reform of the abortion laws. There is a widespread feeling among the community that the laws no longer meet the requirements of society, but they will not be altered until society understands considerably more about the underlying principles which govern our social morality.

Then again, customs vary. Those which are satisfactory in Melanesia are by no means equally satisfactory in France. The attitude of the Frenchman to sex expression is by no means necessarily acceptable to the Englishman or the Turk. However, it is probably true that the principles of sex behaviour in countries like Norway and Sweden, America and England are more developed than those in some other countries. It is unlikely that the principles of behaviour which exist in Russia at the present time would be either acceptable or workable here, although there are certain underlying ideals in the relationships between the sexes in that country which might well be adopted more generally in this country. In some countries, for instance in France, sex experience occurs earlier and is accepted as normal. In England, however, this is by no means the case, and the general tendency is to assume that all sex relationships outside marriage are essentially unwise.

THE MATING AND REPRODUCTIVE ACTS

As the result of more accurate scientific knowledge it is now known that woman has both mating and reproductive needs, and further, that they both require satisfaction. This well-recognised biological law is admirably illustrated by many fishes and insects. In bees, for instance, the male sex and reproductive acts consist in the placing of the sperm in the body of the female, whose sex act consists in the reception of the sperm. Her reproductive act, however, occurs at a much later date, when she lays her eggs which may, or may not, be fertilised by the sperm already placed in her body.[1] We recognise this dual need in woman when we realise that it is essential for her to obtain a satisfactory orgasm during her sexual act, irrespective of whether she desires to, or can, become pregnant.

[1] *Sex*, by Dr. P. B. Wiesner.

The point is stressed because its acceptance is essential if marriages are to be built on a sure and lasting foundation.

Although there is a difference in function between the sexes there is no difference in their basic needs. We are only just beginning to realise, for instance, that when a couple marry their main desire to start off with may be for a completely satisfactory sex union. We have over-stressed the importance of the reproductive side at the beginning of marriage and have not paid sufficient attention to the need for mutual satisfaction. The desire for reproduction should grow naturally from the other; it is, in a sense, a further development. Married couples are often surprised to find how their desire for children grows after they have been married for some months and have perfected the physical side of their mutual life. Only when these two functions have been properly harmonised will the couple become emotionally stable. Most thoughtful married women will maintain that their sex feelings are as strong as a man's, though their feelings vary more in rhythm. Society may have fostered the idea that women were devoid of sex feeling because the consequences of admitting to these feelings were often far more disastrous for women than for men. Until a few years ago the exercise of the sex function in women usually ended in pregnancy. The control of conception has made it possible for women to separate the mating desire from that of reproduction in precisely the same way as in the case of men.

CONTRACEPTION

Whilst it must be clearly recognised that there is a place in our social structure for the proper use of contraceptives, it is equally true that they can be abused. This truism applies to food or gas or morphia. It is not the article or discovery or fact which is evil or bad, but the use to which it is put. The motive behind the action must be positive and directed towards the welfare of the individual and humanity. Contraceptives are intended to be used positively for the spacing of children or for the preservation of the health or life of the mother. When they are used callously, indiscriminately, and without proper thought or understanding of their function and effect, as often occurs in indiscriminate relationships, they are being misused.

A proper knowledge of physical technique is essential if they are to be used wisely. This should be acquired from a skilled physician. Knowledge gleaned from newspaper advertisements, books, and friends is likely to be unreliable, and may result in contraceptives failing in their primary object, namely the prevention of pregnancy. The majority of articles sold are unsatisfactory for one reason or another, and the sooner the public realises it the better. It is possible to obtain a 98 per cent security from suitable methods properly taught.

Finally, there are various forms of "birth control" not involving the use of contraceptives, which are even more unreliable. Men are in the habit of assuring women that coitus is perfectly safe because they know the essential precautions to prevent conception, whereas, in reality, they know very little about the subject. Women should be chary of such statements however charming and delightful the individual who makes them. If they want knowledge they should obtain it for themselves from reliable sources.[1] They are then at least in a position to make up their own minds.

Many people are deeply concerned with the morality of contraception. Is it in accordance with God's purpose for man? Is it in accord with, or contrary to, the natural law?[2] We should be shirking our responsibilities if we were

---

[1] Most doctors can put people in the way of obtaining reliable information if they cannot give it themselves. Failing that, a letter to the Secretary, Family Planning Association, 69 Eccleston Square, London, will suffice.

[2] The natural law means in this connection not the working of the forces of Nature as they are, but the norm of human existence as intended by the Creator.

to avoid this extremely difficult problem. The following remarks, therefore, are made with a view to stimulating discussion rather than with any intention of being dogmatic. They should be read in conjunction with what has been said in the first two chapters.

In these chapters, and indeed throughout the whole book, an attempt has been made to show that an individual is composed of various parts which must function harmoniously together if the individual is to become a *real* personality. These parts or "bodies" are the physical, emotional, mental, and spiritual.[1] They can be looked upon as comprising four storeys of a house. It is necessary for an individual to live on all these four storeys. If he only lives on one or two, or is afraid to go on one of the floors, he is not making the best use of his house; he is not living a fully integrated life; he is not a complete personality. If he lives only on one floor, whether it be the emotional or spiritual, he is not truly balanced; he is over active in some directions and not sufficiently active in others. Even if the individual is living on all four storeys of his house, the house is still not "himself". He is something more than his house.

We have also tried to show that the individual has union with God—the Master-Mind if the reader likes that term better—through the spiritual; it is in the spiritual sphere that he has the chance of immortality. The motive for which we live and strive must be positive and directed towards a higher level of life—a greater maturity.

The end of Man, therefore, is the fullest union with God. This often involves the surrender or redirection of some things for those that are more valuable and permanent. This conception of our purpose on earth does not deny the expression of natural satisfaction. Indeed, these satisfactions are good, and recognised as such by the Church, but most valuable are the fuller and more lasting satisfactions which are obtained through the spiritual. Ultimate development is to be found on this

[1] Graham Howe and Le Mesurier, *The Open Way.*

"immortal" plane toward which we are all consciously or unconsciously striving.

In considering the many practical measures which we employ in this life for one purpose or another, we must ask ourselves whether they are likely to advance or hinder us in our ultimate purpose. Will they enable us to live a fuller and more balanced life? Only if they are beneficial are they in accordance with the natural law. In which way does contraception act? Of course it may act detrimentally. On the other hand, if it is used to enable an individual to live more fully on all four storeys of his house, and so progress towards the ultimate perfection, which is our goal, it must surely be in accordance with the natural law. Nothing hampers spiritual development so much as a misuse or over-emphasis of the physical. Straighten that tangle out; make the physical act normal and satisfactory, and the *whole* personality will develop evenly and beneficially. This is what contraception can and will help to do, because it enables the individual to live his emotional life with balance and reason. That sex can be, and has been, misused in the past is obvious. That sex education and scientific knowledge can and should be welded into the whole life of the individual is the whole argument of this book.

It is possible to look at the problem from another angle. Those who believe in the traditional interpretation of the natural law maintain that the physical expression of sex is only lawful when there is no bar to conception. If conception is inadvisable for any reason the only alternative is abstention. This interpretation presupposes that the only purpose of sex is reproduction. It does not exclude the natural enjoyment of the act provided nothing is done to interfere with conception. It is well to note here that coitus interruptus is just as contrary to the natural law as the use of a contraceptive.

Tho e who do not agree with this interpretation maintain hat there are two important purposes in the sex relationship; the reproductive principle and the pleasure principle.[1] The one should not be stressed to the exclusion of the other. People should have children because it is the purpose of marriage, and they should also enjoy the relationship. That is independently important and not "just a secondary end". There are times when the reproductive principle cannot or should not be exercised. There are times when the pleasure principle alone is desirable as a relief for mutual tension or as an expression of mutual love. If this pleasure principle is not allowed reasonable expression the individual may suffer psychological or even physical damage. It is also maintained by those who hold this view that the sex act must never be expressed unless it is mutually desired. If the woman is disinclined for the relationship, as often occurs naturally on certain days every month, or if she is afraid that pregnancy may occur when for some good reason it is not desirable, the mutuality of the act is not being expressed. For this reason the practice of the safe period is not advocated because the only days in a woman's cycle when it is thought that she cannot, or at least is unlikely to become pregnant, are just when she is least likely to want any physical expression, and she may indeed feel an active revulsion for it. For a man to insist on a performance of the sex act under such conditions is quite immoral.

As a matter of fact St. Thomas Aquinas had a good deal to say about sex relationships and the acceptance of pleasure in that relationship. For instance, in discussing luxury he says: "Sin in human acts is what is against the order of

---

[1] The word "pleasure" is here intended to mean "the healthy expression of passion, the fostering of mutual love, the strengthening of the sacramental bond of marriage," to use the words of a recent Roman Catholic writer. It is not limited to physical feeling. Several people who have kindly read the MSS. of this book have said that the term is unsatisfactory and misleading. Whilst this may be true it has not been possible to find one more satisfactory, indeed the writer feels that there is something to be said in retaining and emphasising the word "Pleasure" because there is an element of pleasure which is most definitely right and needs emphasising. Nevertheless, it is not right unless the additional meaning is included.

reason. Now it is the function of that order to refer every-thing suitable to its own proper end. And therefore it is not a sin for man to make a reasonable use of things for the end to which they were made, in due mode and order, provided that end be something truly good. But as the preservation of the corporal nature of an individual is something truly good, so also is the preservation of the nature of the human species an excellent good thing. Now as the use of food is directed to the preservation of the life of one man, so is the use of sexual intercourse directed to the preservation of the whole race of mankind. And there-fore the use of sexual intercourse can be without sin, done in due mode and order as is proper to the end of human generation."[1] Here is a definite acceptance of sexual intercourse in marriage as being right for its proper end, namely marriage and human generation. So far there would be no disagreement between the most rigid theo-logian and the more modern view point. St. Thomas then goes on to say that: "Abundance of pleasure in an act, when the act is directed according to reason, is not con-trary to the golden mean of virtue. And besides, it matters not to virtue how much pleasure the exterior sense feels; that depends upon bodily disposition. What does matter is how the inward desire stands affected to such pleasure. Nor from the fact that simultaneously with such pleasure reason can have no free play for the consideration of spiritual things, can it be shown that the act in question is contrary to virtue. Mere occasional interruption of the act of reason for some purpose according to reason, is not contrary to virtue; otherwise it would be contrary to virtue to go to sleep."[2]

This passage gives definite sanction to the pleasurable side of the sex relationship in marriage, but should be read in conjunction with the former one by which it seems obvious that there must be intention of having children.

---

[1] *Aquinas Ethicus*, Z.53. Vol. II, trans. Joseph Rickaby, p. 324 (abridged). Burns & Oates, 1896.
[2] ibid., p. 325.

In other words, the motive must be directed in the right way. Here again there would be no disagreement between the two schools of thought. It would be fair to say that the rigid theologian would say that whilst this passage obviously accepted the pleasure principle it ruled out contraception because the proper end of human generation was being frustrated. There can be no doubt that a literal interpretation of the passage would mean that, but here again the passage must be read in the whole context of St. Thomas' thought. It could be argued, and this would be the writer's position, that provided there was an intention to have children at some time, as, for instance, when a couple were spacing their children properly, contraceptives would be used rightly and with "reason". And further, that science has accumulated evidence to show that we must pay far more attention to those aspects of the physical relationship not directly connected with generation than has been understood in the past. The knowledge we possess concerning these two matters is new and did not exist in those days, so St. Thomas could hardly be expected to legislate for them. It can be argued that the use of contraceptives for the purpose of achieving "abundance of pleasure in the act" is quite definitely "according to reason". Those who formulated the law at that time could not have had the knowledge because it was not known, any more than the function of the sex hormones was known. They undoubtedly acted with the best possible intentions, but that does not alter the fact that our new knowledge gives us a wider and more comprehensive understanding of the whole sex function in life. This new knowledge should be accepted by the strict theologian and incorporated in religious teaching. So far as the writer is aware, there is nothing in the writings of early moral theologians to prevent their acceptance and indeed St. Thomas' words can be taken as an indication that they should be accepted.

Thus the Church is faced with a new problem which cannot be solved by old formulas, however good and valuable they have been. In order to deal with this new situation constructively, we must devise principles which may necessitate the broadening or revaluation of our interpretation of the natural law. We waste valuable time which might well be spent in constructive work because so many people try to treat the problem as if it has existed in the past and was already settled, whereas in actual fact we have hardly begun to consider it constructively.

The upholders of the modern viewpoint agree with the traditional interpretation of the natural law in that the sex act must not be used selfishly; and that children are the natural outcome. But they also maintain that there are obvious times when a woman should not become pregnant, as, for instance, when pregnancies would be detrimental to health or where there is every chance of the child inheriting disease. In such cases, the pleasure principle should not be denied expression. The whole question really comes down to that of motive. If the motive is good and directed towards the ultimate development of the personalities of both partners; if they are enabled to live on all four storeys of their house, then there can be no valid objection to the employment of contraceptives and the use of the pleasure principle.

It is clear that in this new interpretation of the natural law its scope is very materially widened. Both reproduction and pleasure are necessary to a full life. They can be combined; they may be separated. Every couple will have to decide their attitude in accordance with their own consciences because the organised body of religious opinion does not feel the situation is, as yet, sufficiently clear. It is to be hoped that they will not delay too long because a positive indication of their attitude which really embraced these new factors would be of immense help at the present time.

It is possible that a solution will be found on the question of motive. If a couple are having children, or intend to have children, there should be no objection to the employment of the pleasure principle during such times as pregnancy is inadvisable, for reasons satisfactory to the consciences of the partners concerned.

No apology is offered for the length of this discussion. The problem is fundamental and its solution is essential if we are to have any positive advance in moral reconstruction. Of one thing we may be certain. Scientific contraception has come to stay. It is one of the most valuable discoveries of the age and possesses infinite possibilities for constructive use in the formation of a stable family life.

CHOICE OF PARTNER

Young people frequently choose the most unsuitable partners. A man who requires considerable sex expression will often choose a woman whose attitude is such that he might have realised that she would never meet his needs. Similarly, a highly sexed girl will choose a man who has little interest in physical matters. It is not easy to explain this behaviour. Many people think they can teach their partners to make love more efficiently or to take more interest in sex matters, ignoring the fact that people are differently constituted; that it is physically impossible for some people to show much emotional feeling. It ought to be possible for an intelligent couple to determine whether they are likely to suit each other in this respect. A man who rarely kisses his fiancée, or even avoids opportunities for the simplest love-making, is unlikely to make a satisfactory partner for a normally sexed girl. He may be physically immature or psychologically inhibited. In either case marriage between the two is likely to end disastrously. Similarly, a man who finds that his approaches are resisted or turned aside should think twice before committing himself. It is true that he may have more chance of awakening real emotional response in the girl when they are married—indeed, it is part of his duty— but even so the girl should take some interest in love-making.

There are some people who refuse to discuss sex matters, saying that they know all about them or that everything will be all right when they are married. In such cases there is probably some underlying fear or suspicion of sex which should be removed before marriage. It is dangerous to take a chance with something so essential to a successful marriage. If one person continually refuses to discuss matters the other should refuse to go on with the relationship until the problem is sorted out.

FAMILY RELATIONSHIPS

Many of the difficulties between parents and children are due to the inability of parents to realise that their children are growing up; have individualities and opinions of their own, and a natural desire for independence. Some parents are unwilling to encourage their children to seek free development or follow their natural bent; they try to keep them tied to the parental apron-strings and to force them into vocations and occupations by no means suited to the abilities of the young people. They often adopt grossly unfair means to further their own ends. For instance, to refuse to provide a boy of eighteen or nineteen with a latch-key and to insist on his being in by ten o'clock and giving an account of his doings, is not only unfair, it makes the parents appear ridiculous to the boy. It demonstrates conclusively that the parents are not on such terms of friendliness and intimacy with their children that an atmosphere of trust and reciprocity is naturally created. If children are not unduly subject to their parents they will speak quite naturally about their friendships and activities.

How many parents really encourage their sons and daughters to bring home their friends of both sexes? It so often happens that these youthful affairs have to be carried on in secret, and that the only possible meeting-place is the cinema or street. And yet what is a home for, if not to bring one's friends to, however unsuitable

I c

the friends may appear in the eyes of the parents? The best way of showing a boy that his latest girl friend is of the wrong type, is to give her the run of the house.

Then again, some parents refuse to give their children a reasonable amount of pocket-money and expect them to account for every farthing. Or they will go farther, and deny them financial aid unless they conform to the parental view regarding jobs. It is not suggested that young people may be allowed to embark on any harebrained scheme which attracts them. Rather should the parent-child relationship be conducted on a basis of mutual discussion, sympathy and understanding.

Finally, what of the parents who insist on daughters remaining at home, thereby denying them the chance of an occupation of their own? The reasons for this range from a desire to keep an eye on the girl and to prepare her for marriage, to the view that a daughter does the housework more cheaply than a maid. How stultifying! How grossly unfair! How utterly un-Christian! And yet how common. We may well ask by what authority parents exercise these "rights" over their children. Have they, indeed, any "rights"? Can they expect absolute obedience? Such conditions hardly seem possible in the light of our conception of the development of individual personality.

What then should be the relationship between parents and grown-up children? Mutual respect, friendship, and a readiness to give and take and to co-operate in the running of the home? Assuredly. The relationship of children to parents cannot be based on "filial duties" or "rights". Neither can children ignore all responsibilities towards their parents. If it is true that they did not ask to be born, very few of them would refuse the offer were they in a position to consider it. On the other hand, the parents have probably done all in their power to provide their children with as good an education as possible, very often at considerable sacrifice. The real basis of family relationship is, of course, mutual affection.

Family relationships are, however, profoundly influenced by the close emotional contacts which exist throughout the family. Emotionally we pass through a variety of stages as children. After a primary concern with ourselves we reach the stage when our interest is focused on some object or person, "The highest manifestations of which are found in the passionate and all absorbing loves of subsequent adolescence or adult life."[1] The mother or nurse is usually the first person selected but this attachment is later transferred to the father. The importance of effecting this change satisfactorily cannot be over-emphasised. Its failure may account for the prolonged affection which may exist between a girl and her mother in an unnatural degree. If only parents and children would be more open with each other; if only they would discuss their mutual problems openly and naturally. It is often difficult to take the first plunge and open the conversation. Once started, however, in a spirit of mutual love, it is comparatively easy to continue. There is need for tolerance and forbearance.

Let us consider one or two particular problems. We must understand, first, the child's recognition of his own inadequacy, his weakness, and his need for security. This does not mean that he must be defended from every possible danger; that he cannot go out because he may catch a cold, or run because he may fall. This type of "Security" is really repression; it is unnatural because every child has a life-plan, a goal, and an urge to reach that goal, *which must be allowed to develop*. As man is a social animal needing to live in community with his fellow-beings he must possess an urge to develop his social feeling. "It is always the want of social feeling which causes an insufficient preparation for all the problems of

[1] Prof. J. C. Flugel, *The Psycho-analytical Study of the Family*, p. 14.

life."[1] The less social feeling possessed by an individual the more imperfect, insecure and inferior does he feel. The child must therefore be encouraged to escape from the family apron-strings, to launch out for himself, to climb trees, build bridges, ride bicycles, and generally venture forth on his own. But he will not do so unless he feels he has a secure home to which to come in time of trouble. His need for steadfast, confident and loving parents is vital. The more secure he feels in his home surroundings the more will he be willing to launch out on his own, realising that his parents are always there, ready and willing to help, guide and counsel. Without this security he will have no courage.

We possess a dual capacity—an urge to advance and a desire to return to the infantile state. The more we retreat, the more self-centred we become and the less social feeling we possess. Such people lack courage for the tasks of life. They are hesitant, uncertain of their reception at the hands of others. They imagine that people are looking at them, picking them to pieces, criticising them and disparaging them, and as a result they are afraid to go out and enter into ordinary social occupations. They are happier reading, or going for a solitary walk. They are reticent and indecisive in business, shy and reserved in sexual behaviour, retiring and afraid in society. Many men would be far more satisfactory husbands if they could only develop greater social feeling. This does not mean a greater avidity for dances or cocktail parties, but rather a real feeling of responsibility for socially valuable work.

Many young people lose their sense of security owing to the way in which their parents quarrel. They will sense the antagonism between the parents even when it is not outwardly apparent. Night terrors, bed wetting, excessive nervousness, unruliness, or even excessive goodness may be caused by this feeling of insecurity. Some children cannot sleep until their parents come home; others must

[1] Adler, *Social Interest*, A Challenge to Mankind, p. 10.

have a light in their room, whilst others are unnaturally good and obedient through fear of being taken away by the policeman or the postman, or of being shut up in a room or cupboard. In some cases it is suggested that either the parent or even the child itself will become ill or die if it does not follow a particular course of action. All these things lead to a sense of insecurity which is often manifested in adult life as restlessness, inability to concentrate, morbid fears, stuttering, or inferiority. If young people find themselves troubled with these matters they should obtain expert help because the matter can be put right.

THE PAMPERED CHILD

One way in which parents bring about this unsatisfactory state of insecurity is by pampering their children. The child trying to pull itself from one stair to the next, is struggling for perfection and independence. It needs encouragement. The feeling of achievement that comes to a child when it has at last reached the top must be immense. If it is always carried by a fond parent, for fear that it may fall and hurt itself, it will eventually expect to be carried up. It is so much easier to let someone else do the job for one. If this type of parental behaviour is extended to all the activities of life the child will very quickly develop a life-pattern that is built on dependence upon others. It will create an entirely false set of values for itself and will become noisy and objectionable when it is not attended to immediately by its parent. It will make such demands on the parent that it will become parasitic, "constantly putting other people under contribution for its needs".[1] Such a child has lost all incentive to struggle for life and development. When it reaches the larger life of the world it is unable to fend for itself and retreats from life. Its retreat is complete when it commits suicide.

[1] Adler, ibid., p. 119.

Pampering is one of the worst evils that can happen to a child, and one from which many of us have suffered in greater or lesser degree. The parent, usually the mother, is afraid of losing the child's affection and therefore does everything possible to retain it. No true bond of affection was ever forged on this footing. The parent-child relationship will only develop and persist through life if the parent encourages the child to courageous growth and the development of social feeling. Only then will the child naturally love its parent. A child's true emotional response cannot be demanded as a right; it can only be given spontaneously as a result of both recognising the independence of their personalities.

Excessive sternness (usually on the side of the father) is another serious parental fault, which may even amount to actual deprivation and want, although this latter condition is more often due to social conditions and economic distress. The result, however, is much the same, namely, the development of an individual devoid of social feeling and largely concerned with the satisfaction of his own instincts. Having lacked pleasures in early life he makes up his mind to have them when he grows up; to him, pleasure becomes the only goal worth striving for. Of such material is the young criminal made.

A child must be treated as a personality. His life pattern is formed in early years so that young parents must do everything in their power to provide him with the chance of independent development against a background of intelligent, loving security. A child is sensitive to atmosphere and can sense discord and disharmony as well, or better, than an adult. How important therefore that the parents should be mutually adjusted.

These matters are vital to an understanding of ourselves and our family relationships. Recognition of a type of upbringing will often enable an individual to understand his own difficulties and problems, and will provide him with a clue to the better conduct of his home life.

OTHER RELATIONSHIPS

Much trouble arises in the parent-child relationship because of the parents' refusal to recognise that as the child grows it necessarily desires affection and friendship with other people. This is particularly apparent in the refusal of a mother to accept a daughter-in-law or a father to like a possible son-in-law. There are problems of adjustment here for the parent, in which the child can often give much help by showing particular thought and consideration, trying to bring the parent into the relationship rather than to keep him out. There is need for considerable tact and forbearance on both sides if a satisfactory result is to be obtained. It is, however, well worth striving for.

Family quarrels generally occur because one or both of the individuals concerned refuses to allow that measure of growth and development which is natural, and because they cannot speak openly and without anger. Frank and quiet discussion, conducted with a real desire to understand the others' point of view, will often bridge the gulf that divides youth from age. In particular, children must realise that they have duties to their parents; they should try and spend some time at home, if possible in active co-operation with their parents in some mutually satisfying occupation. In all difficulties the parents must ask themselves whether the objections they raise are sincere or due to possessiveness, whilst the child must assure himself that his proposed course of action is not just self-interest. The parent must encourage the development of a positive life-pattern whilst the child must not refuse emotional response and affection.

GRAND-PARENTS

Children who have grand-parents are usually lucky. There is nothing more delightful than to see an understanding grandfather or grandmother discussing the affairs of the day with a youngster. The relationship between these two generations is particularly attractive and happy, besides being of great value to the young people. Considerable understanding and sympathy is exhibited by the old to the young and is often greatly valued by both. There should be no grudging of this affection on the part of the parents. On the contrary, it should be welcomed and fostered.

SEX AND THE FAMILY

A great source of difficulty in family life is the inability of parents to discuss sex matters with their children. We can only touch briefly on the reasons for this condition. The original fault almost always lies with the parent who has, at some time or other, failed to deal openly and adequately with the childish questions that were naturally asked. This in itself can often be traced back to an unsatisfactory parental sex-life. If the parents have failed to sort out their own problems they are likely to possess such strong guilt feelings that they will be unable to deal with their children's question rationally. They escape by refusing to discuss the subject, by a denial of its existence, and by reactions of shock or painful silence when the subject is mentioned. This sense of guilt can be transferred to the child without a word being spoken.

In many cases, however, the parent is painfully aware of his or her inadequacy and would welcome an approach from the child, who, if he has passed the adolescent stage, may be in active need of help or guidance. A few well chosen words at this time might break down reserve and enable the two to talk sensibly and rationally, thus bringing them much closer together. There are some parents who, however willing to talk to their children, find it impossible to do so. They should at least see that the child is put in touch with someone who can be trusted to give adequate information in a plain, straight-forward manner.

LOVE

No word in the English language is so full of meaning so beautiful and yet so greatly misused as the word "Love". We talk of parental love or brotherly love, of the love life of a sexual debauché or the love of adolescent youth; of physical and spiritual love. The list could be extended indefinitely. It is a pity that we have not other words with which to refer to some of these conditions. Is it possible to define Love? Does it mean something different for each of us? Is it just the term for a certain emotional state which has a different context according to our experience of life, and the stage of emotional development we have reached?

There is no doubt that there are various types of real love. Parental love, for instance, is a real and lasting emotion, quite different from the love of a husband for a wife, or the love of friends. Physical attraction, or sympathy, or ecstasy is not love. Love is a state of mind, and is always expressed in personal relationships. The love of a child for its mother is, in the main, a possessive, self-seeking love, perfectly natural to the very young, but unnatural if prolonged in the same form to adult life. The love of a man for a woman may be a possessive, self-seeking emotion embodying little more than sexual feeling but, in its fullest development, it is completely unselfish and directed almost entirely towards the well-being of the one loved.

Love is never truly expressed until it is free from possessiveness. It demands an equal sharing with another; "of accepting and being accepted", as Professor John Macmurray puts it. "We do not love a person if we only want that person for ourselves. Sex relationships under such conditions are definitely immoral. Even if there is mutual desire this is frequently concerned with self-gratification and does not necessarily mean that we love each other; that we want to express ourselves totally in the other and with the other; that we are concerned with the development of the personality of the other." [1]

Here then lies the crux of the matter. The creative unselfish aspect of the relationship must always be to the fore. The thought of each individual must be towards the other. Adler tells us that being in love is being in that state of mind when one thinks of and for the other person. This requires the exercise of intelligent thought, the understanding of physiological and psychological principles, control, regulation, and re-direction of energy. It is diametrically opposed to the idea of "romantic love" visualised by so many couples, as a state of wonderful bliss into which they automatically fall and which endures indefinitely without any particular effort on their part.

Psychologically speaking, love is a sentiment, that is to say an organisation of our various emotions about a particular object. Love includes mental, spiritual and physical qualities. We cannot divorce one from the other two and call what remains love. Thus there is a difference between fascination and love. A relationship in which the satisfaction of our own sexual feelings is uppermost is not Love, it is more akin to the biological state of lust or to the immature emotion of childhood. Again, if we are chiefly concerned with the avoidance of sexual experience or with the acceptance of physical attentions without contributing anything to the relationship, that is not Love either.

Only when our main concern is the satisfaction of the other person and the development of that individual's personality are we approaching the state of real Love. It is probably best to regard Love as the combination of a biological urge, an emotional state, and an attitude

[1] *Reason and Emotion.* The chapter on the virtue of chastity is one of the best things that has been written on this subject.

of mind which is moving from the self to the outside world.

Let us repeat that Love is active co-operation with another for the benefit of another. It is being in a state of charity towards one's neighbour. It includes unselfishness, tenderness and truth. It necessitates the development of social feeling. It requires all the help that science and religion can give to make it fruitful. It demands the exercise of the very best that is in us in unselfish service.

If that definition is not sufficient we can take another and fuller one that includes the fundamentals of Christian teaching and the deepest psychological truths:

"Though I speak with the tongues of men and angels and have not charity, I am become as sounding brass, or a tinkling cymbal. And though I have the gift of prophecy, and understand all mysteries, and all knowledge; and though I have all faith, so that I could remove mountains, and have not charity, I am nothing. And though I bestow all my goods to feed the poor, and though I give my body to be burned, and have not charity, it profiteth me nothing. Charity suffereth long, and is kind; charity envieth not, charity vaunteth not itself, is not puffed up, doth not behave itself unseemly, seeketh not her own, is not easily provoked, thinketh no evil; rejoiceth not in iniquity, but rejoiceth in the truth. Beareth all things, believeth all things, hopeth all things, endureth all things. Charity never faileth; but whether there be prophecies, they shall fail; whether there be tongues, they shall cease; whether there be knowledge, it shall vanish away. For we know in part, and we prophesy in part. But when that which is perfect is come, then that which is in part shall be done away with. When I was a child, I spoke as a child, I understood as a child, I thought as a child; but when I became a man, I put away childish things. For now we see through a glass darkly; but then face to face; now I know in part;

but then shall I know even as also I am known. And now abideth faith, hope, charity, these three; but the greatest of these is charity."

CHAPTER VIII

SEXUAL MALADJUSTMENTS

The imagination of a boy is healthy; and the mature imagination of a man is healthy; but there is a space of life between, in which the soul is in a ferment, the character undecided, the way of life uncertain, the ambition thick-sighted.

JOHN KEATS. 1795-1821

WHEN WE TALK about a normally sexed individual we mean a person whose sexual emotion is directed towards, and activated by, someone of the opposite sex. This wide definition includes the man or woman who is potent but whose sexual energy is so latent that very little effort is made to find a sexual mate, and the couple whose sexual activity is naturally satisfied at monthly or weekly intervals. These different types, and many more besides, come within the norm and can be partly accounted for by variations in hormone activity. When we come across people, however, who are not interested in the opposite sex and only find emotional excitement and interest with people of their own sex we are dealing with a different category.

·As the ultimate purpose of sex is the union of two people of the opposite sex for their mutual benefit and the propagation of the race, we are unable to class this type as normal. On the other hand, it would be unfair to call people with homosexual tendencies perverts, because we all pass through a homosexual stage. It is better to regard homosexuality as an abnormality—a deviation from the normal. Its origin is closely related to hormone action on the one hand and psychological factors on the other. Its better understanding is another example of the value of scientific investigation as opposed to the earlier negative teaching that everyone was either male or female; if you do not belong to the first category you must necessarily belong to the other. In actual fact not one of us is either completely male or completely female. In order to understand this, we must know something more about biological and psychological principles. Our forefathers made grievous mistakes because they did not have the knowledge that we possess to-day. Not only did they think that everyone was either male or female, but they thought the sexes were antagonistic to one another, whereas in fact they are complementary. We all possess some qualities of the opposite sex in greater or less proportion. We are all striving for completeness by union with the opposite sex. How does this come about? Let us consider the biological aspects first of all.

A consideration of sex determination will help us to understand the problem better. What is it that decides whether a child shall be male or female? It used to be thought that sex determination depended upon the female— upon some constituent of the egg or even of the ovary itself. This is now known to be incorrect. The female cell— the egg—is unable to move by itself and is indeed a neuter as far as sex determination is concerned. Left to itself it would remain female if it began to grow and develop. It needs the activity of the mobile male cell or sperm to bring about any change towards masculinity. Male cells are now known to be of two types, X and Y. If a X bearing sperm unites with an egg the result is a female (XX). If a Y bearing sperm unites with an egg the result is a male (XY). It is possible that science will eventually be able to separate these two types of sperm so that we shall be able to deter- mine the sex of children by introducing the required type of sperm into the uterus by means of artificial insemination. In the first weeks of life the developing embryo is neither male nor female; it possesses both qualities. If it develops towards maleness, the male sex organs will grow larger; if towards femaleness the male organs will remain rudimen- tary. What is it that determines whether male or female will ultimately develop? The answer is the male sex hormones. Left to itself the embryo will become female. Stimulate it with male hormones from its own sex glands and it will become male. Experiments have been done which prove that it is possible to alter the sex of a female rat, for instance, by injecting male hormones. It is equally possible to remove the male sex organs, which produce the male hormone, in which case the individual will revert to the female type. As Kenneth Walker puts it: "The female may therefore be regarded as the basic type of the mammalian species, and the male as the more highly differentiated type derived from it by the action of the male hormone. Man may be considered, therefore, as derived from woman rather than woman from man. The myth of Lilith and not the story of the Garden of Eden is the better parable of man's birth. He, and not woman, represents Nature's second thoughts, the more specialized type, the rib taken from the woman's side and shaped into the likeness of a companion."[1] But the hormone action of the sex glands is not the whole story. Many other glands, such as the pituitary, are concerned in this process. Nevertheless, the main principle is clear.

Should the male hormone be inadequate for some reason or other, as for instance, if one of the male sex organs is a testicle and the other an ovary, and should the secretions of both these glands be functioning actively the individual might become an intermediate type—a hermaphrodite. Thus an individual may have the secondary sex characteristics of the female—breasts, internal genitalia, etc.—and yet one of the primary sex organs or gonads may have testicular tissue in it and be functioning in a masculine capacity, although insufficiently to turn the individual completely towards maleness. In such a case the surgeon is justified in removing the male organ, thus allowing the unrestricted development of the female characteristics.

[1] *The Psychology of Sex*, p. 28. Penguin Series, 1940.

It is obvious that there must be many gradations between the complete female type on the one hand and the complete male type on the other. It is in this way that homosexuality may develop. Given the right soil, that is to say an individual in whom the male hormone is not acting with great intensity, add to it certain environmental and psychological influences, which tend to retard still further the normal male development, and it is possible to produce a homosexual individual in whom emotional interest and response is only aroused by one of his own sex.

Authorities differ in their definitions of homosexuality. Dr. William Brown, for instance, says that there are two forms; the first, in which a person takes on the characteristics of the opposite sex in his sexual life and plays the more passive feminine role and is the object of attraction for the second and more active type, who is outwardly indistinguishable from a normal member of his own sex.[1] Others talk about congenital and acquired types; the congenital applying to the passive form and the acquired to the more active form. These latter distinctions are not strictly accurate because it is unlikely that any homosexual conditions could be acquired unless the right soil was present. If the hormone action is weak and the adverse influences begin very early in life, the condition is akin to the "congenital" type.

It is usually easy to recognise this congenital or passive type because we find certain feminine traits well developed. The whole structure and make-up of the individual is slim and fragile, tending towards femininity. Such people are frequently artistic, musical and highly intellectual, and their interest in women from an emotional point of view is practically non-existent. To them a woman is as dull emotionally as a male is to a heterosexual man—more so in fact. Their sexual energy is inverted. They are difficult to cure because there are deep-seated psychological factors superimposed on the physical condition.

[1] *Psychology and Psychotherapy*, p. 129. 1940.

This is a misfortune which may be remedied as scientific knowledge increases. That the male homosexual should be penalised legally and run the risk of imprisonment for his "offence" whilst the female counterpart is ignored, is a hardship that can and should be remedied.

Active homosexuality is more difficult to understand. To all outward appearances the individual is a normal healthy male capable of taking an active part in all male activities and games. And yet he is an active homosexual whose only sexual interest is in people of his own sex. The influences that bring about this condition are deep-seated and probably originated in early life. They are largely psychological and are directly concerned with the individual's relationship to his parents and home. Such cases are also difficult to cure. If this cannot be effected much can be done to help the person to understand and accept the situation, thus enabling him to conduct his life in an orderly and disciplined manner.

ADOLESCENT HOMOSEXUALS

There is another type of homosexual activity, which is often called homosexuality, said to be prevalent in public schools and brought about by the segregated condition of the sexes found in these and similar institutions. School-masters themselves frequently refer to the "homosexual problem" in schools by which they mean something quite different from the passive or active homosexuality we have been considering. It would be well to find a new name for this type of case because a good deal of muddled thinking exists because people do not make it clear in their conversation to which condition they are referring. It is proposed to call this type of activity—adolescent homo-sexuality—because it is really little more than a habit occurring in the adolescent phase of development.

We have already seen that, psychologically speaking, we pass through a stage of normal homosexual development. Were it not so we would be unable to make healthy friendships with people of our own sex. We have also seen that our development may be arrested at different stages of which the homosexual is one. This is particularly liable to occur at or just after adolescence. Outside influences may be brought to bear on the young individual, which will encourage him to think and act as if he were homosexual. In such cases of adolescent homosexuality it will usually be found that the individual is really heterosexual, but has latent homosexual tendencies which can be brought to the surface and developed. One of the great dangers of this situation is that the real active homosexual may teach his or her practices to the young heterosexual and thus create an appalling muddle or tension in that individual's mind. It is necessary, therefore, to guard against the possibilities of this occurring by directing young people's minds in the right direction and by giving them sufficient knowledge to enable them to spot the individual who is endeavouring to tamper with their emotional life. Even here, however, it is probable that a certain type of "soil" must be present.

There are many young men and boys in whom the male hormone is not acting with great strength. The shy, introspective youth who likes to be by himself and finds it difficult to make friendships easily and who is none too good at games and masculine pursuits is just the type who may be swung towards homosexuality, if the environmental conditions are favourable. Another boy of the same age and under the same set of circumstances would probably be unaffected by the homosexual influences simply because his male activity was so strong that they would pass over his head. The "homosexual" practices in schools are rarely of a true homosexual nature and more often than not take the form of mutual stimulation or self-stimulation. It is a mistake to call the people who carry out these practices homosexuals. It is possible that some of them may become active homosexuals if the practice is persisted in, but in the majority of cases this is a passing phase which is rapidly displaced by normal heterosexual activities

Kc

as the boy grows up and leaves school. It is at this stage that intelligent and helpful guidance can be most useful.

The real homosexual does not usually show himself at this stage. If he is conscious of his feelings he keeps them to himself, but in the majority of cases he is only dimly aware that anything is amiss.

Segregation of the sexes undoubtedly plays a great part in the development of mutual stimulation as it does of self-stimulation. It is no uncommon thing to be told by boys that their troubles are minimised or non-existent during the holidays, when they are freer and more likely to mix with people of the opposite sex. Another and important incentive to these conditions is the lack of any effective emotional outlet at school. Any sign of affection between people of the same sex is frowned on and instantly suppressed. This is unnecessary and unfair. It ought to be possible to allow and even encourage normal healthy friendships and leave it to the good sense and understanding of the young people to suppress anything in the nature of active physical expression should this arise. This will only be possible, however, when there is a far more satisfactory educational system regarding sex matters. The lack of satisfactory education is one of the main reasons for the prevalence and over-emphasis of this problem in our schools. Boys know next to nothing about their physiological growth and development; about the action of hormones or the stages of psychological growth through which they must necessarily pass. Neither do they understand anything about the nature and purpose of sex or the physical manifestations of normal sexual growth. They are unaware of the significance of self-stimulation and frequently start the practice out of curiosity. Only in the rarest cases are they "evil-minded", in which case they are probably pathological. Curiosity in the young is a natural condition which should receive adequate satisfaction by proper instruction.

Teaching and explanation will do much to enlighten

and help them. It is possible to show them that sex is a dual relationship which involves another person of the opposite sex and must never be used in such a way as to harm the other individual either physically or emotionally. Friendship also is a dual relationship in which there is equal responsibility for the welfare of the other. If the energy which they possess and the natural attraction which they feel for their friend is directed towards the benefit of that individual—towards mutually creative interests in games and occupations, for instance—there is nothing wrong with their friendship. Indeed, it is beneficial and stimulating. If the activity is directed towards physical expression it is obviously being directed towards noncreative ends and is likely to harm one or both of the people concerned, just in the same way that sexual activities may be misdirected in heterosexual relationships.

It will be seen, therefore, that to speak of homosexuality in schools is a misuse of terms and really creates confusion of thought, because true homosexual manifestations are rarely apparent in schools. The writer has had considerable opportunity in recent years of investigating conditions in schools owing to the fact that it is his privilege to visit a good many public schools every term for the purpose of giving some help and guidance in the principles of sexual behaviour. Whilst he has come across cases of self-stimulation and mutual stimulation he can only recall four cases of a more serious nature in which there was a definite homosexual tendency. In none of them was the condition obvious, nor had they indulged in any "homosexual practices" nor been "spotted" by the masters.

This approach to the adolescent problem is one which is often found useful in dealing with the active homosexual. In many of these cases it is impossible to subject the individual to a long course of analysis, nor is it at all certain that the analysis will cure the condition. It is, however, important to relieve the tension in the patient's mind and enable him to recover faith and confidence in himself. It is necessary for him to understand what homosexuality is and to accept the fact that he is homosexual. This in itself is a difficult task, but once accomplished makes him happier and more certain of himself. It is then possible, by illustrating the principles upon which heterosexual relationships should be founded, to show him that he has the same responsibilities towards people of his own sex, and should never act in a manner detrimental to the personality of another.

Whilst we have concerned ourselves mostly with the problem as it affects the male it must be remembered that the same situation can and does arise in women and girls and must be dealt with along similar lines. In order to make the picture complete we must add that some people are bi-sexual; that is to say that they are attracted to both sexes. Here again, the same principles hold good and an attempt must be made to direct the energies of the individual towards one or other of the sexes; preferably, of course, the opposite sex.

PSYCHOLOGICAL INFLUENCES

We must now consider the psychological and environmental influences which affect the individual in early life and may weigh the balance in favour of homosexuality. We have seen that normal sex interest and activity are developed by regular stages. The infant is self-centred and finds sex interest in the activities of its own body. This interest gradually widens until it includes other individuals of either sex and finally becomes localised in individuals of the opposite sex. This normal development is subject to interference by outside influences which may have a profound effect upon the temperament and personality of the individual. The psychological energy may become repressed into the unconscious, in which case it may show itself in various strange and abnormal forms, or it may be redirected into channels not directly concerned with sex, but on a higher plane of activity and having a definite social value.

The baby, for instance, must adjust itself to its environment and give up its self-centredness and take interest in others. If its upbringing is stormy and difficult so that it feels insecure and frightened it may remain in a state of self-admiration which may develop into a definite narcissistic pattern in which the individual is incapable of loving any one but himself. This attitude, created in the very earliest years of life, may persist throughout life and form a large part of the homosexual constitution.

The various influences which affect the individual act on the mind by suggestion. They are either expressed actively in words or more insidiously by the whole environmental surroundings of the individual. For instance, let us suppose that a sensitive child, whose physical make-up tends to the feminine type, is told by his companions that he looks like a little girl; that this suggestion is frequently repeated, and that, to further increase his difficulties, his mother not only thinks and says that he is a "pretty, sensitive child" but even dresses him in girlish clothes for several years beyond the baby state. She probably keeps him very near her, never allows him to do anything for himself, and is always shielding him from real or imaginary dangers. She certainly keeps him away from his boy friends, whom she considers play and behave in a very rough manner. Every thought, word and action tends to overprotect, coddle and turn him into a hothouse flower. What is the result? As he grows up he realises that he is not exactly like other boys, that he does not like their games or manners, and is happier at home with his mother or playing by himself; that he is frightened of men and manly talk. By brooding over these differences and magnifying his difficulties he becomes even more introspective and lonely, and visualises his problems as abnormalities. Adolescence and the physical changes which normally occur at this time, merely increase his difficulties. Indeed, it may be that his physical development lags behind that of boys of his own age. Being of a feminine type the male hormone is probably not acting so strongly within him as in others. If he is twitted by his companions about this immature physical development, he naturally imagines that he is even more abnormal than he really is. He becomes even more unhappy and loses confidence in himself and his own masculinity. Because masculinity demands approach to and interest in the opposite sex he finds it almost impossible to make the necessary adjustments that will bring him into contact with girls in a normal and natural way. He thinks that because he is strange, his "abnormality" will be spotted by the girls, whom he accordingly avoids, seeking refuge with those of his own sex. Thus not only is he emotionally immature but all the factors in his character and environment have tended to retard his normal development and produce a vicious circle from which he is unable to break away. If nothing is done to help him, he is likely to become a homosexual of the passive type.

It will be obvious that many varying influences have caused this condition. There has been the original soil; the fond stupid parent, whose one idea is to shield her darling from the dangers of the world; the silly unintelligent chatter of his friends; and the vicious circle of his own fears. The whole situation may be summed up as follows: "The masculine man will always need as his complement a feminine woman; the man who is not very masculine may be attracted by someone masculine, i.e., another man. The feminine woman will fall in love with a masculine man; the somewhat masculine woman may find her complement in another woman."[1]

Homosexuality of the more active type is likely to owe its origin to acquired psychological factors which again may have their origin in the parent-child relationship rather than in lack of effective hormone action. It is, therefore, more likely to be cured. Some people may feel

[1] Gordon, Harris and Rees, *An Introduction to Psychological Medicine*, p. 207. O.U.P., 1936.

that much homosexuality is inevitable and that the feminine type of child must necessarily develop into a homosexual. This is not so. The true congenital or passive type is comparatively rare, but the psychological conditions in the home and school environment that bring about the more active type are very common. They are counter impulses to the developing sexual interest and activity of the child and are "the result of social pressure—that is to say, the result of the influence of the human environment. This influence is manifested, not merely in direct precept, in warning, in punishment, in expressions of disapproval or disgust, but in the whole system of secrecy, of significant silences, of suppressions, of nods and winks and surreptitious signallings, of sudden causeless snubs and patently lame explanations amidst which such sexual interest as the child possesses has to find a modus vivendi and an intelligible meaning."[1] It is hardly surprising that such influences, to say nothing of the active quarrellings and bickerings that go on between parents in the presence of their children, is sufficient to swing the balance of their emotional development from the normal to the maladjusted. Nevertheless, in spite of all these difficulties, the vast majority of homosexuals can be helped to a greater or less extent even if such help can do no more than make them realise their state and encourage them to exercise the same restraint and control, which should be the basis of a heterosexual existence. Our views regarding the treatment of homosexuality, therefore, need radical alteration. There are, of course, other sexual maladjustments such as frigidity and impotence, but it is not intended to say more about them than has arisen in discussion in other parts of this book. There is one matter, however, about which we have acquired considerable knowledge and that is what Havelock Ellis terms "polyeroticism". As it plays a great part in modern sexual behaviour it is necessary for us to understand its meaning and application.

[1] W. Trotter, *Instincts of the Herd in Peace and War*, p. 82. 1919.

POLYEROTICISM

We have had occasion to point out that there are two underlying purposes in the sex relationship. The first is reproductive and is the predominating principle amongst women. A woman's life is not complete either physiologically or psychologically until she has had children. This does not mean that women who do not marry and have children cannot or do not lead happy, useful lives. Of course they do. Nevertheless, the principle remains that the desire for home and children is a strong, compelling force in the lives of the majority of women. Indeed, we can go farther and say that neither men nor women are complete until a happy and permanent relationship is established with a member of the opposite sex. That is what we are all striving for. The second purpose is the performance of the sex act, which is the predominating principle in the male, in whom the sex act and the reproductive act are included in one and the same functions; coitus produces sexual pleasure and children. The same cannot be said of women. Coitus may result in children with sexual enjoyment; it may equally result in sexual enjoyment without children. The compelling urge that attracts most men to women is sexual pleasure. The desire for children comes later. Many men do not want children, neither do they like their wives to be pregnant, nor the baby when it comes; not until they actually see it and play with it and watch it grow up. Then the paternal feeling in the man is really awakened and he delights in his child and wants another. Much of the early activity of marriage is concerned with the adjustment of these two angles. The man, as we have already seen, has to accept the fact of parental responsibility and love for children; the woman has to recognise that sexual pleasure is a strong element in the marriage relationship and must be accepted and enjoyed for its own sake.

Ideally speaking, both the man and the woman should

accept these ideas in principle before they marry, recognising that the motive for their marriage is twofold—sexual pleasure and reproduction. Both women themselves, and society as a whole, have tended to ignore the importance of the pleasure principle and have failed to equate the physical with the other factors in the marriage relationship, with the result that, having achieved very little satisfaction, the woman quickly becomes bored with the relationship. This means that the man does not derive very much pleasure from the one-sided relationship and tends to look for satisfaction elsewhere, or else omits the love play, which is a necessary preliminary to any sex act, merely performing the act as a relief for physical tension. In such cases there is very little relief of real *emotional* tension for either partner, with the result that considerable strain is often set up, which shows itself in many curious ways which seem to have no direct relationship to sexual activity. It is in such cases that one finds the woman permitting coitus because she thinks the man needs it, but deriving no benefit from it herself. In fact, the reverse may happen because the act appears boring and unnecessary and therefore creates a tension in her mind, which may or may not be recognised. The man meanwhile becomes more introspective and self-centred.

Such cases are frequently seen in the consulting-room and their cure is often very difficult because the couple have frequently fallen out of love with each other from the physical point of view, although they may have much else in common which holds them together. The prevention of the condition, however, is a much easier affair, and one of the chief ways of bringing it about is the acquisition of suitable knowledge regarding sexual technique before marriage.

A couple cannot be expected to know all these things by instinct, nor can they acquire all their knowledge from books, although many of the latter are very helpful. In cases that have been properly instructed before marriage, or at any rate in its early days, one is impressed by the fact that the couple return happily to the relationship after the birth of the baby, knowing quite well that they possess a mutual bond which can be renewed and developed to their mutual advantage. Two facts, however, need to be stressed at this point.

The first is that the woman may take several months to regain her former attitude and sensation owing to the fact that her primary concern for some time after childbirth is with the baby and its needs. The other is that the element of romance and variety must not be allowed to die out. It is here that the man has an important part to play because he must always be thinking out new ways of making love to his wife. He must remember that the first glamour of the relationship has passed away; that there is a new member of the family to be thought about and cared for, and that the economic situation may be such that his wife may have more to do and more to think about and cannot perhaps give him her full attention, to say nothing of the fact that she may be tired.

An intelligent couple will think out these problems together and find a working arrangement that is mutually satisfactory.

One of the mistakes that people make is to have sex relationships too frequently. It is far better to have a well thought out enjoyable relationship once a week or once in ten or fourteen days than to have a hurried relationship two or three times a week. Although such behaviour may have been both possible and satisfactory before the birth of the child it by no means follows that a similar situation will be possible afterwards. The man, therefore, will have to exercise considerable forethought and control whilst the woman will have to appreciate his thoughtfulness and help him with all her power. The demands made upon her at this time are numerous and complicated, for not only does she often have to look after the house, buy and see to the food, tend the baby and be attractive to her husband when he returns in the evening, but she also has to be ready to listen to his troubles, go out with him occasionally to friends or amusements and satisfy his physical needs. Truly a difficult but by no means impossible task, as is proved by the numerous women who accomplish it successfully.

The dual purpose of the sex relationship that we have been discussing has been considered by Havelock Ellis in some detail. With his usual insight he has pointed out that the reproductive purpose of the relationship is the parental aim and that the pleasurable and mutually satisfying purpose is the erotic aim. "Without the factor of mutual love the proper conditions for procreation cannot exist; without the factor of procreation that sexual union, however beautiful and sacred a relationship it may be in itself remains, in essence, a private relationship incomplete as a marriage and without public significance."[1]

We have said that if the sex relationship becomes unsatisfactory or never develops satisfactorily from the pleasure or erotic point of view, the man will tend to find someone else who will perhaps satisfy this side of his feeling, and we have shown that there is a fundamental reason for this in the man's make-up. Some confusion of thought has arisen over this matter and indeed still exists, because people conclude that man's nature is such that he needs two or more wives; that he is, in fact, polygamous. But this is not the case. Men do not want more wives; they are probably quite happy and contented with the wife and family that they have. But they do require satisfaction for the pleasurable side of the relationship; they are in other words polyerotic. That is to say they want, or tend to want, more sexual freedom. If they cannot find this satisfaction in marriage they will seek it elsewhere. The same thing applies to women and has become more noticeable recently. In a mutually adjusted relationship the problem will not arise for either partner, and in any case it is more a man's problem than a woman's, because the woman tends to find happiness and satisfaction in her children and home.

[1] *Studies in the Psychology of Sex*, Vol. IV, p. 508. Random House, N.Y., 1936.

Although a man may be polyerotic, this does not mean that he is promiscuous, which means that he has sex relationships with women quite indiscriminately. Nevertheless, if he does not find his basic needs satisfied in the home, he may have various affairs with women in his search for the woman who will satisfy the erotic side of his nature. When he finds her, he is likely to remain faithful to her. Thus we find the underlying reason for the married man having a mistress. The situation is well summarised by Havelock Ellis.

"It would seem that most persons, women as well as men, are monogamic and polyerotic. This is to say they only desire one permanent marriage, but they do not find that the relationship stands in the way of sexual attraction to one or more other persons, though the attraction thus aroused may be felt to be of a different nature to that experienced for the permanent partner, and it may prove quite possible to hold such attraction more or less in control. There appears to be no sexual difference in this matter. Women are fully as well able as men to experience affection for more than one person of the opposite sex, though on account of the deeper significance of sex for women they may be instinctively more fastidious than men in sexual choice, and on account of social and other considerations more reticent and cautious than men in manifesting or in yielding to their affection."[1]

The possibility of putting these ideas to practical use has naturally been made more possible by the introduction of modern contraceptive methods and has thus created one more problem for society to deal with.

Whilst the problem of homosexuality has been considered mainly from the male point of view the same problems arise amongst women. If sex education is necessary for boys it is equally so for girls, many of whom have the most rudimentary ideas about their psychological development, although they may be better informed about menstruation. Information on this matter, however, is

[1] Havelock Ellis, *Psychology of Sex*, p. 242. Heinemann, 1933.

by no means all that is required. It is essential that the young woman should appreciate sexual differences and the varying needs of both sexes. Many girls are frightened of accepting the feminine role because they do not rightly understand it. Being afraid of growing up, they tend to fix their friendship on older people of their own sex. An unhappy affair may encourage this reaction. The results are very often disastrous to the girl's emotional life, more especially if she comes in contact with the masculine type of woman who has refused or been unable to accept her femininity and has adopted the male role as a defensive mechanism. In such cases we have all the ingredients for the development of a homosexual relationship.

Some adolescents are worried because they experience dreams of a homosexual nature. This is of no significance provided it is recognised that the individual is still in the homosexual stage from which he will make natural progress. If they persist and appear abnormal in any way they should, of course, be investigated.

CHAPTER IX

BETROTHAL AND MARRIAGE
PREPARATION

Love warms and illumines life when truly tended.
SIR JAMES CRICHTON-BROWNE. 1840–1938

WE HAVE ALREADY suggested that some system of betrothal might be adopted by the Church and society as a solution of our difficulties. Let us consider the matter further.

The first criticism that might be levelled against this suggestion would probably refer to the statement that there should be no children. It would be argued that no contraceptive is 100 per cent safe. This is questionable now because contraceptives have improved. There is considerable evidence available that modern contraception can be 99 per cent secure and the only reason one cannot say 100 per cent is because it is impossible to guarantee that the woman will do as she is told. In other words, there is no reason why, in the situation we are considering, where all people would automatically receive expert advice, there should not be a 100 per cent security.

Let us ask ourselves again if there is any evidence that society and the Church has ever accepted the idea of betrothal which included sex union. This would really be an acceptance of trial marriage, with certain important additions, of which there is much evidence as to its antiquity and universality. According to Ploss and Bartels trial marriage consists "in the peculiar custom of a betrothed couple living a regular life of sexual association for a certain time, sometimes even for several years, the marriage being definitely concluded only if, during the trial period, the fiancé succeeds in making his intended bride pregnant. If there is no impregnation, it is assumed that these two people are incompatible and they then leave each other. Not infrequently the girl forsaken in these circumstances very soon finds a fresh suitor, who willingly goes through a new trial period with her. For a man to leave a girl whom he has made pregnant in such a trial marriage is considered particularly shameful, and he is subjected to the contempt of everybody."[1]

It must be noted that the purpose of the relationship is to ensure the fertility of the woman, whereas in the situation we are considering children would not be permissible until the couple were satisfied that they had made no mistake. If this principle were accepted, there is no reason why the couple should not pass through a further stage in which pregnancy was the determining factor. If this was found to be impossible for some reason or other the final vows need not be taken. There is much to be

[1] Ploss and Bartels, *Woman*, Vol. II, p. 218.

said for allowing infertile marriages to be dissolved and this system would tend to eliminate the possibility. If pregnancy occurred marriage would then follow. There is no reason why society should not accept such a state. It might go far to improve social morality, and would at least provide an organised and well-thought-out plan.

There is much evidence to show that pre-marital intercourse was permitted and regarded as normal in many different societies and countries.[1] Pope Alexander III issued the decree "that of two brides, the real wife was she with whom the betrothed man had already had coitus".[2] It was well recognised in Germany as late as 1912 and there is considerable evidence of its existence in our own country at the present day. It is by no means uncommon to find that when a couple "walk out" they frequently have sex union and when the girl becomes pregnant the man marries her. This old established custom has its origin in the need for the man to make sure that the woman he has chosen is fertile and will provide him with children to work his land and provide for his old age. The early Christians did not invent any special marriage service; indeed it was many years before the Church adopted one. For early Christians it was sufficient to attend church after the civil ceremony.

It seems, therefore, that there is evidence, from various different sources, that sexual union was recognised as a preliminary to marriage. It was not, of course, organised or conducted along lines which would be acceptable to-day. Indeed, the fact that a custom was prevalent in former days is no argument for its continuation or revival at present. The old customs were not carried out in a manner which would be scientifically acceptable to-day. On the other hand, there is no reason why we should not adapt the custom to suit our present needs. There is no direct evidence that it was condemned by Christ. Can we not draw a parallel between this practice and that of the traditional

[1] Ploss and Bartels, *Woman*, Vol. II, p. 217.
[2] ibid., p. 219.

Christian attitude to the whole sex question? In neither case had they the knowledge that we possess to-day. If our attitude to the one needs readjustment why should we not say the same of the other?

Closely allied to this question is the problem of defloration. The theological attitude to marriage to-day is that neither the man nor the woman should have had previous sex experience. Thus the woman is a virgin, that is to say a person in whom the hymen is "unbroken". It is the husband's duty or privilege to rupture or destroy the hymen. It follows from this that the use of contraceptives by the woman is impossible and undesirable. Indeed, many doctors say that it is impossible to fit a woman with a contraceptive appliance before marriage and therefore advise the use of a condom in the early days of marriage, if pregnancy is to be avoided. Other people go farther and say that there should be no bar to conception to start off with and that contraceptives should only be used after the birth of the first child. We have already pointed out that there are objections to this procedure. Quite apart from this, however, it is incorrect to state that a woman cannot be fitted with a contraceptive before marriage. It is perfectly possible and indeed advisable. It is accomplished by a preliminary dilatation of the hymen, which is equally advisable and makes the performance of the sex act easy and painless. It is well known that this dilatation or defloration is a very old custom and has been practised in almost every country in the world. Here again we are only adapting old customs to modern needs.

The establishment of some system of public betrothal which would be an advance on trial marriage, because it includes the teaching and instruction we have advocated in this book, and is accepted by society as a normal preliminary to marriage, is something which should receive the serious consideration of society. Its adoption by the Church might do much to improve social morality and give official sanction and positive direction to a custom very prevalent in all social groups. That the suggestion is contrary to our present ideas is obvious but that does not mean that it is necessarily bad or incapable of being incorporated into our religious and social system. We must re-emphasise, however, that an intelligent system of early marriage preceded by teaching would meet the majority of our problems.

Let us examine this question of marriage preparation more closely. Considerable stress has been laid upon the necessity and value of obtaining expert medical help before embarking upon sex relationships. Only the minority of people go to the doctor before marriage to make sure that they are even physically fit. Fewer still have the courage and intelligence to seek a more thorough examination or to demand information on sex matters. And yet much can be done, given time and an understanding physician. The visit should be made a month or six weeks before the marriage date, and each partner should arrange to see the same doctor both separately and together.

It is advisable to choose the doctor carefully; the knowledge and capacity he or she possesses for dealing with the subject is of great importance. If the individual's own doctor is not able, or willing, to deal with the matter an inquiry addressed to the Secretary of the Marriage Guidance Council[1] or the Family Planning Association[2] will bring an answer explaining how help can be obtained.

A review of the family history and a physical examination are of course essential at such an interview. Minor conditions of ill health are often discovered and appropriate steps can be taken to remedy them. The suitability of the couple to have children can be gone into and the problem of family spacing discussed; tests can be made to ensure that neither is suffering from venereal disease if this seems advisable. Finally, considerable help can be given about physical technique and contraception, which will help the couple past many pitfalls and give them every chance of a satisfactory relationship.

[1] Mrs. Hume, 13 Wildwood Road, Hampstead, N.W.3.
[2] 69 Eccleston Square, London, S.W.1.

La .

Such information should be available to all sections of the community irrespective of wealth or social status. This would be possible through an extension of the work of the Women's Welfare Centres. A few of these centres are now prepared to give some, at least, of this information, or to tell applicants where help can be obtained. In this way the whole population could be provided for effectively. The establishment of Marriage Guidance Councils in different areas in conjunction with the Women's Welfare Centres and local doctors and parsons is one of the most satisfactory ways in which this problem can be dealt with, until such time as the work becomes part of the general public health programme of the country.

SEX AND SOCIETY

We can no longer consider the problem of personal behaviour from an individual point of view. It is impossible to avoid its wide sociological implications. A variety of social ills are rearing their ugly heads pretty persistently and demand attention. Some people are worried by the possibility of an immediate fall in the population, or with the unbalanced manner in which the social groups are reproducing themselves. Others are more concerned with the undoubted increase in sexual freedom, the rising evidence of abortion and divorce, and the dangers of indiscriminate contraception. Others again feel that there is a deplorable lack of moral tone and that our standard of values is deteriorating. From whatever angle we view the situation the result is the same; we do not possess any constructive policy. Even if we appreciate the difficulty we are divided as to remedies, and therefore do next to nothing.

Is it impossible to reach agreement? Can we not agree, for instance, that it is essential to strengthen the family unit in every possible direction? That to do this effectively we should institute a real policy of planned parenthood in which the best stock in every social group should be encouraged to breed, whilst that which is bad to worthless should be eliminated? In the past those who were socially or physically undesirable were likely to die out through their inability to contend with the trials and tribulations of life. Nowadays owing to the introduction of humanitarian ideals and to our increasing ability to maintain life, these undesirables are preserved in comparative comfort and even enabled to propagate their kind. In addition the flower of our manhood is constantly depleted by war so that the country is in danger of being populated by an ever-increasing number of people who are socially undesirable and incapable of appreciating their personal or social responsibilities. Surely the time has come for us to concern ourselves more with the generations that come after us, lest we destroy their heritage through our own inertia.

Having got so far can we not go a little farther and agree that in order to build up a race of men and women mentally, physically and spiritually mature, we must widen our educational system and concern ourselves more with ultimate values based on scientific knowledge and psychological principles, realising that the dissemination of biological knowledge—however important in itself—is of little value unless it is accompanied by sound principles of personal behaviour. We must try to bring about a radical change of thought amongst the masses of the population, directing our efforts to all sections of the community—to child and parent, youth and adult—in a variety of different ways.

Finally, is it not simple common sense that marriage preparation must become a recognised part of preventive medicine in which the whole community must co-operate? Can we not therefore set up bodies capable of dealing with these problems all over the country so that the public can easily obtain reliable information without undue expense?

These ideas are not impossible; they demand thought, planning, and money. It seems ridiculous to suggest that the country is not rich enough to spend a few millions each year on this type of social service. Unless something drastic is done within the next few years the situation will become a major problem affecting the whole future of our civilisation.

CHAPTER X

THE FUTURE

> Those actions are esteemed virtuous which are thought absolutely necessary to the preservation of society, and those that disturb or dissolve the bonds of community, are everywhere esteemed ill and vicious.
>
> JOHN LOCKE. 1632–1704

BEFORE ANY REAL improvement occurs in moral behaviour we must do the following things:

1. Think out our ideals and principles afresh.

2. Abolish the unsatisfactory conditions of social life which make it impossible to live up to any positive ideals or act in accordance with free principles.

3. Educate the public to a sense of their own responsibility.

In order to make any positive progress we need a new spirit and a new aim. The spirit must be that of unselfish co-operation and the aim a planned society in which each citizen co-operates with his fellow men for the good of the whole community. The centre from which all our various activities must radiate and to which all our thought and care must be devoted is the family unit. Thus, a healthy and stable population is essential. In order to achieve these ends we shall have to replan the whole of society. Planning does not mean regimentation, as we see it under the Nazi rule, but rather the co-ordination of our social structure in such a way that individual freedom will be preserved. It means the planning of the railway train but not of the conversation that goes on inside the train, to use an illustration given by Professor Manheim at a recent conference on education in Oxford.

Let us consider shortly some of the social problems that will need our attention before we can hope to find a real improvement in social morality. As we have suggested that the creation of a healthy and balanced population will be our main task let us look at this aspect of the question in more detail.

THE FAMILY AND POPULATION

We have seen that there are deep-seated psychological reasons for saying that men as well as women should be concerned with the family and should learn to accept the responsibilities, limitations and joys which that state demands, if our personality is to be used to the fullest extent. If we want to stabilise marriage and the family we should take steps to make marriage and all that it involves easy and possible. This is precisely what we are not doing. As Dr. Noel Harris says: "In civilised countries to-day owing to social economics, very few people can get married until many years after puberty, and moreover, according to social ethics the sexual act is taboo out of marriage and so at once the individual is placed on the horns of this dilemma. Either he must control this urge and not allow this all-powerful instinct to be satisfied for many years after its full development or else the usual urge is satisfied at the cost of a sense of shame, guilt and revolt against social ethics."[1] It is obvious we are not facing up ·to this situation. We have seen some of the evil results which follow the policy of laissez faire.

It can, of course, be argued that marriages are on the increase and that the birth rate has risen slightly in recent years in spite of the mournful prophecies of the experts to the contrary. Whether or not this is permanent cannot yet be determined with any accuracy, but any rise that has

[1] Noel Harris, *Modern Psychotherapy*, p. 11. John Bale, 1939.

occurred is certainly quite insufficient. "It has been estimated that the war of 1914–18 resulted in about half a million fewer babies being born than would have otherwise seen the light."[1] Who can say what will happen in the present war, if it lasts for some time? In all probability the birth rate will fall still farther. In addition, the knowledge of contraceptive technique will percolate throughout all sections of the community to an even greater extent than was occurring before the war, if for no other reason than that the several million young men now in our fighting forces are all receiving information about the prevention of venereal disease, which necessarily includes some information about contraceptives, because one of the most universal methods of contraception—the male condom—is also one of the most valuable preventatives of venereal disease. Again, whether we like it or not, this is inevitable and indeed desirable, because no one wishes to see an increase in venereal disease which, even before the war, took toll of about 60,000 new cases every year.

Professor Carr Saunders has pointed out that "We are not only not reproducing ourselves but are between 25 and 30 per cent below replacement rate". And Dr. Enid Charles has calculated that if fertility and mortality figures continue the same as in 1933 the population will have fallen below 20 millions within a century. Here again it is impossible to say whether the situation that these two eminent statisticians visualise will come about, but there can be little doubt that we are bound to have a reduced population.

The real question, however, is not only how are we going to minimise the fall but how can we ensure the birth of the most suitable stock? The public seems very unwilling to face up to the fact that we are breeding dysgenically, that is to say the best stocks are dying out and the less satisfactory elements in the population are being allowed to propagate indiscriminately.

[1] Eleanor F. Rathbone, M.P., *The Case for Family Allowances*, p. 50. Penguin Series, 1940.

As far back as 1926, Lord Buckmaster gave the House of Lords the following comparison of the birth rate per thousand married people under the age of 50:

Schoolmasters	93
Clergy of all denominations	102
Doctors and Professional Men	103-5
Skilled Labourers	153
Unskilled Labourers	247

There is no evidence that these proportions have altered and so we are entitled to conclude that children are not evenly divided amongst the various social groups. We must not conclude, however, that the children of skilled and unskilled labourers are necessarily unsuitable members of society. That does not follow at all. The important point is that the doctors, clergy, schoolmasters and professional men are not producing their full quota, and no one will deny that they have produced children in the past who are of particular value to society. Their production should be increased, not diminished. In addition, we have a "social problem group" in this country of some four million people—about 10 per cent of the population—which contains a large proportion of insane people, epileptics, paupers, criminals and so on, to say nothing of the mentally deficient people—of whom there were thought to be about 300,000 in 1929—two-thirds of whom can breed quite indiscriminately. As these undesirables come from all sections of the community it is important that we should think in terms of social groups rather than of classes. Professor Carr Saunders points out that within each social group "at one end of the scale there is material of the highest value and at the other end material which is poor to worthless. There is evidence that families are largest within the classes at the wrong end of the scale."[1] Then again there is evidence that the average mental capacity of the population may be declining because

[1] *Eugenics Review*. April, 1935.

the production of children is not evenly distributed throughout the country. This is admittedly a controversial subject
about which specialists differ. More research is necessary
but this requires money for which neither the public nor
the authorities appear to appreciate the necessity. And yet
as Dr. Caradog Jones says: "Intelligence is the supreme
gift which raises man above the level of the beasts."[1] It
would be a grave national disaster if we lost the capacity
for creative thought or the ability to appreciate altruistic
ideals because of our lowered mental intelligence. Only
a small proportion of the population appears to have a
really high intelligence quotient. This is not, of course,
the whole story. There are many other complicated
factors involved and it is only fair to say that some of
these views are by no means universally accepted. This
fact, however, should stimulate further research because
the matter is obviously very important.

There is yet another side to the picture. J. L. Gray, in
his book, *The Nation's Intelligence*, asks if "all individuals
displaying superior ability receive the opportunity to use
it to the best advantage of society?" He proceeds to show
that there is evidence of much waste in intellectual ability
amongst the masses of the population. "The fear of racial
degeneration is widespread in England. It would not be
unfair to say that it arises mainly through the enormous
current under-valuation of the intelligence of the poorer
classes."[2] It seems that in London there are more able
children in the Central Schools than in all the fee-paying
schools put together. "Yet practically none of them have
the opportunity of entry into the professions and the higher
ranks of the business world enjoyed by those who attend
secondary or public schools."[3] In other words educational
facilities are still largely regulated by the parental purse
rather than by the child's ability. "Whatever we do we
must redress the social grievance that arises owing to the

[1] *A Social Problem Group*, ed. by C. P. Blacker, p. 224.
[2] J. L. Gray, *The Nation's Intelligence*, p. 89. Watts & Co., 1936.
[3] ibid., p. 95.

preferential encouragement of more prosperous children in the selection of individuals for higher education in schools within the ambit of state control." [1]

These various facts and opinions are presented here because they show clearly that in this vital respect our social policy is based on false premises. Indeed, we are entitled to ask whether we have any policy at all regarding the type of person who is being born or in the selection of those that are most likely to benefit by our educational facilities. It is true that attempts are being made to remedy the situation with regard to education, but they appear to be very inadequate. With regard to the production of population it is probable that we are, as yet, doing next to nothing. It seems, therefore, that not only is our population likely to fall considerably in years to come but that the best elements in it are not being encouraged to breed, nor is the best advantage being taken of the material we do possess.

Whilst it is arguable that a sex relationship may be the private concern of individuals, the same cannot be said of marriage and children. Many people still feel strongly that marriage is a private affair, and the concern of no one but the two individuals who enter into the contract. To suggest that their behaviour should be directed by any outside person or body, even with regard to marriage preparation, is to them a violation of individual liberty. To interfere with their production of children would, therefore, be an even greater insult. This attitude is as widespread as it is illogical and anti-social. The individual, if rightly educated, should accept the fact of responsibility and co-operation with other individuals for the good of the community. Any action, therefore, which is contrary to the social welfare is dysgenic and contrary not only to psychological principles but to Christian ethics. In a society, however, which sees fit to ignore these considerations, we cannot very well blame individuals for acting according to their own ideas. The institution of marriage is seriously

[1] J. L. Gray, *The Nation's Intelligence*, p. 102. Watts & Co., 1936.

weakened by the indifference of society to these matters. A further menace to the family unit is the abortion problem.

ABORTION

It is generally recognised that all sections of the population are attempting to limit their families by some means or other. We have already indicated that the production of children is by no means fairly distributed throughout the various social groups. The methods of contraception vary in type and effectiveness in different groups. The vast majority of the poorer sections of the community rely on a bad method—coitus interruptus—because it is the cheapest and least troublesome. Its failure rate, however, is very high and when it fails the individual often resorts to abortion which is a most dysgenic procedure. "It has been estimated that between 300 and 400 abortions occur every day in Great Britain, of which the Inter-Departmental Committee estimates that 40 per cent only are criminal."[1] Taussig has estimated the number of abortions in America for 1931 at 700,000 of which 50 per cent were criminal,[2] and he states that one-quarter of maternal deaths in America followed abortion and three-quarters of these deaths were due to puerperal septicaemia.[3] Dr. Kopp in her analysis of 10,000 case histories found that nearly one in every three pregnancies in America resulted in total loss. There is evidence that in this country abortion is most common amongst married women who have had more than four children and there is little doubt that the maternal death rate and infant mortality rate rises with successive pregnancies. In the Report of Maternal Mortality in Scotland for 1935, it is stated that "the death rate from all causes increased with multiparity, reaching in those with nine or more previous pregnancies a death rate twice as high

[1] Dorothy Thurtle, *Abortion : Right or Wrong*, p. 16. Werner Laurie, 1940.
[2] *American Journal of Obstetrics and Gynaecology.*
[3] *Abortion.* 1936.

as the average ".[1] In the same report figures are given to show that the percentage of maternal death rate for abortion was 44 for the first pregnancy, and 340 for the ninth. And as for the infant death rate, Dickinson and Bryant state that out of every thousand live births, 105 babies die as the result of the first pregnancy, 137 at the seventh and 182 at the tenth. Examples and figures of this nature could be produced ad infinitum.

There is considerable evidence to show that those who limit their families by satisfactory methods have more live births and less abortion than those who do nothing. It has been shown by Dickinson and Bryant in America that babies born after more than two-year intervals have an average death rate of 92 per thousand, whereas those in the same group born with less than a two-year interval have a death rate of 147 per thousand. In fact, there is evidence that those who practise effective contraceptive methods have more live births than those who do not. Thus the provision of efficient contraceptive facilities throughout the country under medical supervision would go far towards abolishing abortion and its attendant evils —ill health and a falling population. A carefully thought out policy of family planning which provided for a proper distribution of children to give three or four children per family, together with early marriage and a selection of those people for parenthood who are likely to produce the healthiest children in both mind and body, is therefore one of the matters we must concern ourselves with after the war. Our aim must be the production of healthy children of good mental capacity, whose parents are able to provide them with adequate nourishment and a good home life.

POVERTY AND FAMILY ALLOWANCES

One of our greatest social enemies is poverty. It breeds everything that is bad—abortion, ill health, and anti-

[1] *Report of Maternal Mortality in Scotland, 1935*, p. 67.

social individuals. Of all the methods suggested for its relief the provision of family allowances appears the most practical. Miss Eleanor Rathbone's little book, *The Case for Family Allowances*,[1] should be widely read. It puts the whole position very clearly. Whether or no the State should provide for all the children in the country as Miss Rathbone suggests or whether it would not be better for the various professions and businesses to organise their own schemes cannot be discussed here. The point we wish to make is that, whilst it seems obvious that some form of allowances for children should be made so as to relieve the grinding poverty that is so prevalent the problem is not as simple as that. If the State pays, the State should have a say in the quality of the children produced. We do not want to encourage the production of unhealthy children, although it is obvious that those children who are born should receive the best possible care and education, irrespective of their social group or physical and mental conditions. Miss Rathbone says that children are an asset to the State. They may also be a burden. It has been computed that the cost of educating a mentally backward child is £36 as against £12 for a normal child for the same period. [2] Thus family planning must go hand in hand with these other reforms.

The only way in which these reforms can be brought about is by creating a public opinion which will expect individuals to live up to certain standards and conform to certain ideas and regulations designed to improve the quality of the nation. These regulations cannot be forced on the people—the people must learn to impose them of their own free will. Hence the paramount importance of education. It should become the accepted policy of all social groups that they produce mentally and physically healthy children in adequate numbers and properly spaced. Abortion should be regarded as a confession of failure rather than a social sin. If an individual refuses to

[1] Penguin Series. 1940.
[2] R. B. Cattell, *The Fight for Our National Intelligence*, p. 47.

conform to the social code of morality, we might well
consider his segregation until he has been cured, because
a non-co-operative person who denies the value of human
personality is as ill mentally as one with a grumbling
appendix.

LUXURIES AND SNOBBERY

One of the great troubles before the war was the high
standard of living. Everything was a necessity and everything was expensive. Wireless sets, cars, money for cinemas,
holidays and week-ends, various amusements and enter-
tainments were considered to be necessities of life throughout the whole community. There is nothing against these
things in themselves, indeed they are beneficial and health-
giving, but they are often obtained at the price of a small
or absent family. As such they are being abused. If we are
to maintain a high standard after the war, it must not be
at the expense of family and children. Luxuries, like everything else in life, can be misused. If they breed selfishness
and indifference to social welfare they are being misused.
The trouble is really due to a false system of values. Money,
clothes and expensive entertaining are all over-rated. It
does not matter if you are a clerk or a duke, you have to
keep up appearances even if your bank balance is over-
drawn and your lands and houses are mortgaged up to the
hilt. The whole system of getting what you have not got
before you have the money to pay for it is morally rotten.
Everyone lives on "tick" nowadays; it is the thing to do.
In fact, the economic situation is such that it appears to
be impossible to do anything else. But it is all wrong and
breeds much unnecessary misery and unhappiness.

WORK AND EMPLOYMENT

This is a vast problem totally outside the scope of this
book, but there can be no doubt that the feeling of insecurity,
which is engendered in people's minds as to the uncertainty

of their maintaining their jobs is a most fruitful cause of family limitation. A hundred years ago children were of value to the family unit; the bigger and fitter the family the more chance had it of making a successful position for itself in society. When the family was dependent upon itself for almost everything that it needed, everyone, however old or young, had some job to do. But these conditions no longer exist. The child is a burden on the family for whose education and maintenance provision has to be made, often for many years. Thus the tendency is to reduce the number of children so as to give them the best start in the world. Those who are interested in this aspect of the problem are advised to read a most valuable study of this subject by Guy Chapman called *Culture and Survival*, published by Jonathan Cape, 1940.

HOUSING

Whilst it must be admitted that the new housing estates have done much to remove intolerable conditions and have been a great boon to many people, it is also apparent that many of them have been badly devised. The people who are moved into them have nothing to do and no facilities for getting about and seeing their friends. As they have never been educated to use their leisure—if they have any—they have not the vaguest idea of what to do with themselves. This situation will right itself in time as the younger generation come to live in these estates. Their better education will enable them to make better use of the facilities provided. There is, however, another aspect of the problem. It has been ably demonstrated "that the consequences of moving low-paid working-class families into better houses may be to reduce their food budgets well below what is indispensable for a healthy life, so that most of them will drift back to overcrowded slums if they get half a chance".[1] Moreover, it is useless to design houses

[1] G. D. H. and M. I. Cole, *The Condition of Britain*, p. 160. Gollancz, 1937.

and housing estates that are so "labour saving" that the cost of light and heat is prohibitive and the inhabitants cannot avail themselves of the facilities. In many cases, of course, the women are so untrained that they do not know how to manage or what to do in their new surroundings. As has already been suggested, communal feeding and communal facilities for recreation and child care would go a long way to encourage the creation of the family.

The fact is, of course, that although there has been a great deal of house-building "only quite a small proportion has gone into the erection of houses which are within the means of ordinary working-class families earning relatively low wages".[1] But the problem is by no means confined to the poorer sections of the community.

The middle classes are constantly hampered by the unsatisfactory housing conditions they have to put up with, whilst the small flat is scarcely designed for family life—certainly not for babies. Neither has education in housewifery kept pace with other aspects of social improvement. There is no point in having uneconomical houses especially when every social group is hampered by lack of effective labour help, and the wife has to devote much of her time to contending with unnecessary difficulties. The English character seems to delight in unnecessary domestic discomfort, a relic, no doubt, of the spartan age of early morning cold baths and no fires in August. It is impossible to expect women to have large families under such unsatisfactory circumstances. Our housing policy wants revising. Perhaps it would be fairer to say that it wants extending and redesigning to provide the maximum assistance in the difficult job of providing and rearing children.

EDUCATION

Closely allied to the housing problem is that of education. We have already seen that much talent is wasted

[1] G. D. H. and M. I. Cole, *The Condition of Britain*, p. 155. Gollancz, 1937.

through lack of educational facilities. Much of the education provided for the upper classes is far too expensive even for the people for whom it is designed and is often wasted on those who cannot reap sufficient benefit from the intellectual diet provided. It cannot be said that the financial outlay involved always provides sufficient return either to the parents or society. It is to be hoped that the war will bring about a better distribution of educational facilities amongst the various social groups. Even although the public schools only provide education for a small proportion of the population, it would be as unwise to abolish them as to do away with the voluntary hospitals. Both have an important part to play in our national life, but there is no doubt that the State will have to enter into a closer relationship with them. This does not mean that the State need assume complete control of the public schools, should it make financial grants to the schools, any more than that the hospitals need be completely controlled by the State because they receive some money from the State. The important thing seems to be to make available to those who are most likely to benefit from it the really valuable teaching facilities to be found in the majority of our public schools.

In discussing the fact that a great deal of the educational activity of the country is being wasted or misplaced, J. L. Gray and P. Pschinsky say that: "In the whole school, population more than 50 per cent of the pupils are denied the opportunity of higher education."[1] Commenting on this situation G. D. H. and M. I. Cole say: "This means that at least half of the superior ability which exists among the children of the British people is either going to waste or is being compelled to fight against immense educational disadvantages in equipping itself for the business of life. No community, however well endowed in the intellectual sense, can afford such waste, without grievous damage to its collective competence in the arts of

[1] "Ability and Opportunity in English Education, " *Sociological Review.* 1935.

life."[1] There seems to be no standardised system of education to which the whole population should be subject, and which, by sorting out the grain from the chaff, would enable the best brains, irrespective of social status, to receive the best education. This is admittedly a difficult and controversial subject which is only touched on here to illustrate the fact that the policy of selection is no more guided by scientific principles than is the production of the material.

All this affects the family in that the "higher" types of education demand considerable financial sacrifices from almost every family that is trying to provide the best education for its children. Many people try to give their children a more expensive education, through reasons of snobbery, than they can or need afford.

What has already been said with regard to luxuries applies with equal force to education. Our educational standards are largely determined by social groups and our purses. If a child obtains a scholarship at a secondary school or the local high school, the whole family standard has to be raised to meet the new social conditions. All the clothes and accessories that are required by the child are frequently out of all proportion to the family income and put a great strain on parental resources. A man gets a rise in pay or obtains a better position in his firm. His first endeavour is to send his children to a more expensive school, not because they will necessarily receive a better education, but because the family will have a better social standing. Much money is wasted on keeping up appearances, in giving innumerable sherry parties and going to expensive theatres and amusements merely because it is the thing to do. If this war teaches us to get down to fundamentals and rediscover what things in life are of permanent value to the individual and to the community, and what are mere social luxuries with which we could well dispense, it will have brought about a beneficial social change.

[1] G. D. H. Cole and M. I. Cole, *The Condition of Britain*, p. 318. Gollancz, 1936.

M c

HEALTH

Let us now consider the health services of the country as they affect the family. We have done much to improve health within the last few years. The establishment of a Ministry of Health and the introduction of the National Health Insurance schemes are probably the two most important advances made in the early part of this century. The health of the nation has undoubtedly improved out of all knowledge, but there are several matters that are of particular interest in relation to family health.

Throughout the whole of the preceding discussion we have had occasion to refer over and over again to the woman and her part in the family system. If the family is essential to the State the mother is essential to the family. She is the most important cog in the whole family system, indeed in the whole national system. What is done for her? How is she provided for? What facilities are provided to make her life easier? The answer is "precious few"! True, there are maternity and child welfare services which relieve her burdens considerably and make child-birth a little easier. Even so, it is by no means devoid of preventable risks.

But the great mistake—in fact it almost amounts to a scandal—is the fact that the mother, the person on whom the whole family system depends, is deprived of the benefits of the National Health Insurance scheme. The reason for this state of affairs is obscure; possibly it is financial. If so, it is a poor reason because the money that is spent patching up the mothers in hospitals and convalescent homes and in many other ways would have been largely unnecessary had they been able to receive adequate treatment in the early days of their illnesses. This is precisely what does not happen. We are still far from achieving a really practical scheme of preventive medicine.

Indeed, the medical profession has not yet realized that its greatest contribution to social betterment lies in the prevention of disease rather than in its cure. As soon as we talk of prevention, we widen the scope of our endeavour and become more socially minded. It is still far too difficult for the average individual to obtain adequate medical attention. The majority of working-class women cannot be bothered to go to the hospital or consulting-room and wait for a long time; they have neither the time, the strength to walk, the penny for the bus nor the odd shilling or two for the "bottle" that the doctor will give them. And what is the use of one bottle of medicine to a woman who has denied herself for so long that her muscles have lost so much tone that they no longer provide adequate support for her organs; whose blood is so lacking in iron and essential vitamins that she has frequent headaches and giddy attacks and is so tired that she cannot masticate the food that finds its way into her mouth, after the rest of the family have been fed. The reader may say that that is an exaggerated picture, but the writer has spent several years visiting people living under conditions which breed this type of woman, even in areas which are supposed to be fairly well provided for by public medical services. The conditions in the "distressed areas" are far worse.

It is not necessary, however, to go to these areas to find almost every possible deterrent to health and family life. There are houses in almost every district that are a disgrace to our civilisation and by their overcrowded and unhygienic conditions are a breeding ground for ill health and every possible type of mental and physical vice. There are places within a mile or two of the Houses of Parliament in which the sanitary conditions are too primitive for words. Damp seeps into the horrible little rooms where paper hangs in strips from the walls; the water supply and cooking facilities are totally inadequate, and the accommodation is so limited that overcrowding is the rule rather than the exception. Of what use is it to teach a woman methods of safe contraception if there is no adequate privacy for her to carry out the simplest technique? What chances have the children of growing up with any decent ideals respecting the sacredness of the body or the value of individual personality? How can health and happiness be maintained in such surroundings?

The truth is that providing no one gets the measles and father does not have an accident or catch the bronchitis and mother does not take too long over having her next baby, things go along fairly well, but once troubles start there is no saying where the situation may end. The whole family organisation may be disrupted with amazing speed. The vast majority of these people are living up to their maximum capacity and have no reserve power to fight off infection. That is why epidemics sweep through whole families so rapidly and often so fatally. It can be argued that there is adequate hospital accommodation, for instance; this may be so in theory but in practice it is not so for two reasons. The first is that the parents frequently refuse to allow their children to be moved to hospital in spite of every effort on the part of those dealing with the case, and the other is that whilst it is true that there are hospital facilities for serious cases there are not facilities for what may be termed preventive cases—the child with bronchitis, for instance, who would get better in hospital in a few days, but remains at home and is ill for weeks, affectionately but inadequately nursed by an overworked mother who has not sufficient money to pay for simple medical necessities. There are still far too many people who think that admission to hospital is the first step to the next world. This attitude can only be altered by more efficient education. The second reason requires a more enlightened policy of public health.

Although there is no doubt that the National Health Insurance has conferred many benefits on the public it is probable that the majority of "panel" doctors are overworked and have not time to give sufficient attention to the minor ills of their patients. It is well recognised by the medical profession that many patients are suffering from conditions which are largely psychological, that is to say they are worried or overworked or suffering from some stress or mental tension, which takes time and patience to discover, to say nothing of the difficulties of correcting or alleviating them. It is just this additional time that the doctors have not got. Anyone who works in the psychological department of a large hospital will agree that many of the minor illnesses and discomforts, the vague aches and pains or even the more serious conditions, are often attributable to disharmonies and tension in the mind. In order to correct these conditions, it is not only necessary to spend considerable time bringing hidden causes to the surface and explaining the problem to the patient, but it is often necessary to enquire into the work and occupation of the patient and devise means for altering or improving those conditions.

It is the mother who suffers most in all these difficulties. However willing the doctor may be to forgo his fee, and there is no doubt that many doctors do an immense amount of work for these people for which they receive practically no remuneration, it is impossible for him to go on doing this indefinitely. Nor, for that matter, do the women desire to receive charity. The result is that the ordinary working woman goes without those medical attentions that are so vital for her. Thus she often develops serious illnesses which might have been prevented had she been able to obtain adequate and earlier help from the doctor. Many women are forced to put off essential operations for weeks or months because they cannot find anyone to look after the family whilst they are away.

We have already suggested that the important problem of contraception is one in which these women are vitally concerned. We have given figures to show that maternal risks increase considerably after the fourth child and that the abortion rate is unnecessarily high. These problems are a constantly recurring worry to the working woman

and are not being met by the authorities. It seems extraordinary that adequate contraceptive advice is not
provided by the public health services now that it is
recognised that contraception of some type or other is an
integral part of our social life. The reasons for this lack
of understanding are attributed to various different
causes by different people. Some say that it is due to
religious opposition; others to the fear on the part of
certain political parties that the liberty of the individual
is being interfered with or that some ulterior motive is
being devised to prevent the working classes from producing
an adequate number of children. There is no rhyme or
reason in these latter arguments, which are really due to
a misunderstanding of facts. Other things being equal,
there is every reason to suppose that the working-class
woman using suitable contraceptive methods would
produce an adequate family, properly spaced and far
healthier than is at present the case. And the abortion
rate and maternal death rate would be materially reduced.
We must presume that the real reason lies deep down
in the warped psychological mechanism of those in
authority, whose minds close up to progressive ideals
when they approach any problem that concerns sexual
behaviour. They belong to the stable-minded or resistive
type that Mr. Wilfred Trotter refers to in his book on
the Herd Instinct. They must be superseded by the more
adaptive mental type before we shall make much
progress.

In this connection some interesting figures were
published recently in the *Medical Officer* for July, 1938.
Out of 264 cases investigated of women using contraceptives
it was found that the following reasons were given for the
practice:—

Economic and desire to provide for existing
      children   136
Restricted accommodation   135
Actual poverty   77

Fear of unemployment 43
Fear of confinement 14
Wish to space or postpone pregnancy 6
No wish for children 2

In addition "92 of the women expressed their regret that the stress of economic circumstances made them feel it a moral obligation to prevent the conception of the children, whom their maternal instinct desired". The investigation was carried out in the Kensington district and the majority of the people were young parents who evidently possessed not only affection for their husbands and families but a sense of responsibility for the future of their children.

It seems, therefore, that there are many forces acting against the family system. Their sum total makes one wonder why women have any children at all. In addition to poverty, difficulties in the labour market, bad and inadequate housing and expensive education, breeding is dysgenic and haphazard; feeding is inadequate and the health services are unsatisfactory. Cheap luxuries take the place of real necessities, thus creating a sense of false values. Many women have too many pregnancies whilst others have too few. The abortion problem is certainly not being tackled. Adequate contraception—which would remedy many of these evils—is neglected or opposed, and medical facilities for large numbers of women, whilst greatly improved, are still very inadequate. The greatest advance has been made in the maternity and infant welfare services. There are very few working women who cannot receive adequate ante-natal attention and efficient help either from a hospital or well trained midwife. The cost of such services is not exorbitant. Further public instruction in the value of these services is highly essential, together with more adequate hospital accommodation and an even better trained group of medical specialists acting in close co-operation with the National Health Insurance scheme.

INFANT MORTALITY

When we consider infant mortality, however, we may well ask ourselves if we are doing all that is possible. In 1893 the infant mortality rate was 154 per thousand; in 1937 it was 58 per thousand—a very considerable drop. Nevertheless, it is pointed out that the mortality rate for very young babies "has not appreciably fallen since the beginning of the century".[1] One baby in fifty dies within a week of its birth, the chief causes being premature and difficult birth, infectious diseases, such as diarrhoea, and congenital causes. A large proportion of these deaths could probably be avoided were the mothers and babies provided with even greater ante-natal care and more skilled medical and nursing attention. The mortality rate of illegitimate infants in 1935 was 60 per cent above that of legitimate infants.[2]

In 1934 the infant mortality rate in Barrow-in-Furness was 98, in Newcastle 84, in Hastings 35 and Reading 42, so it seems that these marked variations must be largely due to the poverty produced by the various unsatisfactory conditions we have been considering. The number of children in England and Wales who died before their first birthday in 1939 was 50 per 1,000 children born—the lowest figure ever recorded.[3]

It may be presumed that this figure could be reduced still further if conditions in certain bad areas were improved. It is no uncommon thing when visiting patients to find the baby being more or less killed by misplaced care and affection. If it has the 'flu or bronchitis or some gastric upset it is usually wrapped in a vast assortment of clothes, placed in its cot in an overheated room amongst all the smells, noises and commotions that are produced by

[1] *Report on the British Health Services*, p. 107. P.E.P., Dec. 1937.
[2] ibid., p. 107.
[3] Mr. Malcolm MacDonald in the House of Commons, Thurs., Oct. 17, 1940.

cooking, other children, friends, and acquaintances who come in for a few minutes to "pass the time of day", and a tired husband who wants his meal and a pipe. Incidentally, the smell of some of these pipes is enough to asphyxiate the entire family—let alone the baby. The invalid is given milk when it needs glucose, aperients when its bowels should be rested, and various broths and foods when it should be starved. As a final incentive to cure it has a cold and sloppy linseed poultice placed carefully on its "little chest". Not that these attentions are not well meant or that the whole family is not intensely concerned with the progress of the illness. Far from it. Mother and father and the eldest child frequently sit up the greater part of the night to provide for the infant's wants and keep the fire going, to say nothing of the precious money that is wasted on a multitude of foods, milks, cough mixtures and stomach cures. And the doctor when he arrives and looks aghast at the accumulated forces so pathetically marshalled against the enemy and yet so woefully inadequate, wonders what on earth to do! Not the least of his troubles is the fact that the parents usually refuse to allow the baby's removal to a hospital, where it can receive the skilled nursing and attention that is so essential. The objections raised to his suggestion vary from the fact that Mrs. Smith's baby next door was "took away and died that night" to the pathetic plea from the mother that "the poor mite would catch its death of cold in that place and she couldn't abear it". If he is strong willed and patient and has the time, the doctor will try and explain the position to the woman; if not, and if in addition he is over-worked and is not sure if there is a bed available in the hospital, he will give a few simple instructions and tell them to send up someone to the surgery that evening for a bottle of medicine. He will then send in the district nurse and hope for the best. She, poor woman, does her best and in many cases certainly saves the child's life. But one thing leads to another and in all probability some other member of the family gets ill. It is no uncommon thing to visit a house in which practically every member of the family is in bed except the mother, who in reality needs a rest more than all the others put together. The point about all this trouble is that much of it is preventable if, in the first place, the public were better educated and, secondly, if there were even greater hospital facilities than at present exist in many districts for these "preventable conditions".

There is no doubt that the infant death rate would be still further lowered if more attention was paid to these matters by public authorities.

The above description is in no way exaggerated. It is the fault of a bad social system and a refusal to face facts. It is a daily occurrence in the lives of scores of doctors during several months of every year and it is the cause of an enormous waste of life in the first year or two. The writer has seen many such cases and the feeling of anger and frustration that rises in one's mind at the appalling waste of human life is difficult to describe, but remains a vivid and unpleasant memory.

The question of hospital accommodation for "preventable cases" does not even seem to receive sufficient attention by such investigators as those compiling the P.E.P. report on the British Health Services who, in discussing the analysis of waiting lists for hospitals state that "if these waiting lists are analysed it is found that they exaggerate the need. The names of many persons are those who do not need or require admission even if they did once. Moreover, whenever there is a critical emergency case a bed is always found".[1] This is true but does not meet the case. The type of hospital accommodation that is required is not for the critical emergency case but for the case that may become a critical emergency one and cannot be adequately treated by present-day medical standards in the home. It is true that the report adds that there is a genuine shortage of hospital beds in Great Britain.

The relationship between the family doctor (who is

[1] *Report on the British Health Services*, p. 256. P.E.P., 1937.

often the Insurance doctor as well) and the hospitals must be strengthened so that he can obtain expert help and advice for all his patients and the latter can feel that there is one person at least who knows and understands the whole family. If it is necessary to employ outside help it should be done under the guidance of the family doctor, who is as important for the future of medical practice as the family itself is for the State. The fullest diagnostic facilities should be available and be made use of by every person in the country who needs them.

THE MIDDLE CLASSES

This discussion has concerned itself so far with the poorer sections of the community because their number is very great and their lot very unenviable. Their position could be materially improved if the authorities liked to make a concerted attack on the problem and spend some of the money—so easily collected in war for human destruction—on methods of human betterment. There is another section of the public, however, and a very important one, for whom little is done. Those people whose incomes are over the £250 per annum mark and are thus ineligible for National Health benefit; the wives of professional men, whether they be black-coated city workers, doctors, parsons or officers, are very badly catered for. The so-called middle classes, in fact, are not getting a fair deal. They fall between two stools because they are neither very rich nor very poor. They cannot afford expensive nursing homes and private nurses, nor are they provided for in the general hospital system. It is true that many hospitals now have private blocks and wards which are intended for this type of person, but such places are as yet insufficient in number and still too expensive.

It is equally true that there are various hospital insurance schemes which do something to provide for their needs, but in almost every case maternity benefit is expressly excluded. Maternity work is undoubtedly expensive on account of the large number of highly skilled nurses and expensive equipment required. It is also true that much valuable work is done in patients' homes by the visiting midwives who are very highly trained. Nevertheless, the modern home does not accommodate itself easily to the birth of children and there is no doubt that a large proportion of young women in the section of the community we are considering are debarred from having children by the difficulties of finding a suitable place in which to have the baby, to say nothing of the financial outlay involved.

At a moderate estimate it must cost at least £50 to have a baby nowadays if the woman wishes to have a room to herself, a doctor and an anaesthetist. Three weeks in a home at £8 8s. od. per week is about £26; medical fees can hardly be less than £20, which only allows £4 for extras and nothing for emergencies or a special nurse, even for a few nights. At the end of that short time the woman is expected to go home and either look after the baby herself; employ an expensive nurse or, alternatively, a half-trained girl. In addition, she very often has to contend with the house and the cooking because of the difficulty of finding anyone willing to help her at the moderate wage she is able to pay. All this needs altering. The solution surely lies in a widespread extension of the maternity hospital service, or of the maternity blocks of general hospitals. Here there should be wards and private rooms at a moderate cost--three to six guineas for instance, and the fees paid for medical attendance should be strictly limited or, better still, included in some form of inclusive charge. There is no reason why such hospitals should not have a carefully selected panel of doctors working on a part-time or full-time basis specially qualified to deal with maternity cases. All the complicated investigations, X-rays and pathological reports that are required should be readily available to any woman, irrespective of rank or financial status. This, of course, will involve the expenditure of public money but there is no reason why the difficulties cannot be overcome if the public demand it and the Government sets its mind to the task.

It was estimated in 1931 from census returns that there were 9½ million families in England and Wales and that two-thirds of these families consisted of from two to four persons. Many of these families could and would increase their size if some of the problems we have been considering were tackled properly and systematically.

STERILITY

Closely allied to this subject and needing the same sort of treatment is the investigation and treatment of sterility cases. It has been estimated that ten per cent of marriages are sterile. That is a high percentage and means that many potential babies are being lost to the country and often from just those parents who are most anxious and suitable to have children. A high proportion of the cases can be cured, some easily and some with difficulty. In some cases prolonged and costly treatment is necessary, both for the man and woman. The public are, as yet, insufficiently aware of the part played by the male in the sterility problem. In a high proportion of cases the man is at fault. People think that ability to carry out the sex act satisfactorily is an indication that there is nothing wrong with the man and that he is therefore fertile. This is entirely inaccurate. Many men are infertile and yet most capable lovers; others are quite fertile but incapable of effective erection.[1]

Various important problems are raised by male sterility. For instance, why should not a married woman be allowed to obtain a divorce if she finds that her husband is sterile and was so before she married. It would, of course, be difficult to prove to the satisfaction of a Court of Law that a man was sterile before marriage, although there is no reason why a man's degree of fertility should not be

[1] See *The Childless Family*, by Edward F. Griffith, for a further discussion on this subject.

assessed before marriage. In fact, there is a good deal to be said in favour of this procedure. It is a very simple process and might save a great deal of future trouble. At present, a woman has no redress if she finds her husband is sterile and yet she may be desperately in need of a child. Occasionally artificial insemination will be successful; the sperm being effective if introduced into the uterus mechanically, but not effective if they have to undergo the hazards of a long and difficult journey. Only rarely do we find that sterility cases are properly investigated. This is largely due to the fact that the apparatus and technique required for successful investigations are not distributed sufficiently throughout the hospitals, neither are there sufficient doctors able and willing to deal with the problem satisfactorily. Nor has the patient the necessary money to spend. If we wish to encourage parenthood we must see to it that cheaper and more widespread facilities are provided for the investigation and treatment of sterility and made available to every man and woman who needs them, either free of charge or at a very moderate fee. Incidentally, the public must be educated to this responsibility and the knowledge that scientific advances have been made should be much more widespread.

It is not only in regard to maternity service that the middle-class woman is at a disadvantage. Illness in the family is an expensive business; an operation is frequently a financial blow from which it takes months to recover. Here again it is usually the woman who suffers and pays. Numberless families are just managing to keep their heads above water. Illness or an unwanted pregnancy changes the whole picture. One frequently hears it said that an abortion is cheaper in the long run. The usual reason the woman contemplates the abortion is economic; the expense of having the child and the expense of bringing it up. One often finds people criticising these women on account of their snobbishness, by which one must presume is meant their disinclination to go into hospital wards and have their babies and operations as other women do.

This is by no means fair, however. The women would willingly go to the hospital if the hospital catered for them. Besides, it is not always hospitalisation that is necessary; the treatment or investigation can often be done at home. But this usually involves expensive nurses, a radiologist and the laboratory for various tests. Here again something is wrong. There should be facilities in all hospitals for all these investigations for every type of patient at a reasonable and graded fee, the doctors, of course, receiving appropriate remuneration either through the hospital or from the State.

THE UPPER CLASS

There is yet another section of the public involved in the question of parenthood, namely the upper class. It would be more correct to use the word "rich" to distinguish this group from the others we have been considering. Their standards are high and if they are going to have babies they expect everything to be done in the best possible manner, regardless of expense. Some of them are, of course, thoroughly selfish—mere social butterflies—who have never grown up. Their one desire is to have a good time, and they refuse to accept the responsibilities of their position. One can find their counterparts in every section of society. And yet if these people are sufficiently stirred they respond magnificently, as is shown by their behaviour during war. Such people frequently pay a couple of hundred guineas for a confinement and it is obvious that child-birth under such circumstances is an expensive business. It is also quite unnecessary—a luxury trade in fact which might well be abolished. In the type of society we are considering, where the working woman pays a couple of pounds all told, and the middle-class woman from ten to twenty pounds, there is no reason why the richer members of society should not be well cared for at an inclusive charge of fifty guineas. Expensive nursing homes and high medical fees should disappear. All women should receive the same skilled attention and a reasonable degree of comfort when having a baby—that is to say, efficient nursing, the attendance of a doctor when necessary and, of course, a properly administered anaesthetic. Her surroundings, whether in a ward or private room, should be clean and comfortable. If she requires a special nurse she should be able to have one irrespective of her financial status. The whole conduct of every maternity case should be based on the welfare of the woman and her child and the effective provision of essentials. If the woman wishes to pay for additional luxuries by all means let her do so.

It is by no means certain, however, that these measures will bring about the desired result. There must be other and more obscure reasons preventing the better off people from having children; expense and selfishness is not the whole story.

FEES

There appear to be two main reasons why specialists charge high fees. The first is the fact that the doctor has to make his money somewhere, and if he works for nothing at the hospital he has to recoup himself from those who, presumably, can pay to see him privately. The second is that the public choose their doctors in a silly manner and frequently go to someone because he keeps an expensive establishment rather than because he is the best man for the job. It would be far better if the specialists were all attached to hospitals to which the general practitioner had access. The patient could then remain under the care of the G.P. This would maintain the relationship between the patient and the G.P., to which most people attach considerable importance, and yet would ensure the patient receiving adequate consultative help. It would also mean that the patient would be more likely to come across the doctor most able to deal with the condition. If doctors were paid by the State the fee problem would be eliminated

and patients could get as much help and advice as was
necessary.

The fee problem is a serious one from the doctor's point
of view. He has been taught from time immemorial
that his first care is for the patient and he is frequently
hampered in his handling of the case by the inability of the
patient to pay the requisite fees. Fees too frequently destroy
the even tenor of medical relationships and disturb the
harmonious friendship which should exist in the medical
profession. Many doctors would be far happier and better
doctors if they were paid a salary by the State and had not
to worry about getting money from impoverished or
parsimonious patients. In actual fact, the proportion of
the population that can pay adequate fees is very small
and it would be far more satisfactory all round if some more
equitable scheme could be devised in which money did not
play such an important part.

If then our aim is to provide effective preventive treatment for women and their families, five things seem to
be necessary.

In the first place an extension of the National Health
Insurance to include all women. Secondly, an extension
and improvement of the hospital system to include preventive cases and easier specialist services. Included in
this must be an extension of the public medical services
in regard to ante-natal and post-natal care, maternity
and contraceptive facilities. Nor must we forget in this
connection that there is a great need for a more widespread
use of our psychological departments. At present, all
psychological work is expensive because the treatment
is necessarily prolonged, but there is widespread evidence
of its value, not only in difficult cases but in the general
run of preventive illness. Many of the minor conditions
of ill health owe their origin to psychological difficulties
which could frequently be cleared up fairly quickly, if
only facilities were available.

Thirdly, a rearrangement of the fee system. Fourthly,
the provision of centres to deal with the family as a whole.

Nc

Various experiments in Family Health Centres, such as the Peckham Health Centre, have been started in different parts of the country; and should be extended. Their purpose is to deal with the whole family; to keep the health of individual members on a high level; to insist on periodical medical examinations and to arrange for or provide any treatment required. In this way much illness can be discovered and dealt with in its earliest stages. In addition, the psychological background of family life is taken into account and many difficulties are sorted out. The Centres usually provide various amusements and recreations such as swimming, dancing, games and other hobbies. There is no reason why such centres should not be attached to various clubs, housing estates, factories and other communal organisations throughout the country. Not only would doctors be required to staff them, but lawyers, educationalists, social workers and nurses would all provide a valuable contribution to the general welfare of the centre. There is no reason why the general practitioner should not become more closely identified with such schemes.

Fifthly, a realisation of the educative role of the doctor in social reorganisation.[1]

To sum up, therefore, we may say that the main factors which appear to be affecting the family adversely are a falling population about which no attempt is, as yet, being made to use scientific knowledge to correct dysgenic tendencies; unsatisfactory educational facilities, which do not allow for the widest use of the latent talents we possess, and the difficulty of feeding, clothing, housing and providing work for more than one or two children. In addition, the place of the mother in society is not given adequate recognition nor are her wants catered for. There is no positive policy regarding contraception, abortion or sex education. Child-birth is far too expensive and the problems of infant mortality and the care of young children up to five is by no means satisfactory. As a result of all these

[1] See p. 200.

factors, late marriage is becoming more common with a consequent increase in indiscriminate and premarital relationships. In fact, our present policy is merely creating those conditions we wish to abolish. What is to be done?

The answer lies in the word "education". We must give widespread publicity to these problems. In addition we must provide a far more intelligent system of education for both children and adults in the principles of sexual behaviour. Various means must be adopted and every possible channel employed. Books, lectures, broadcasting and films must all have their place. If we provide reasonable educational facilities we can then encourage early marriage. Everything points to this as being the wisest policy. Before going on to consider a few practical schemes that are taking shape and might well be extended it may be as well to consider the situation created by the war.

THE WAR SITUATION

Not only does our sense of values alter in war, tending to concentrate on the present to the exclusion of the future, but the future itself seems so obscure and far away that one is tempted to ignore it. A moment's thought, however, will show that this is a short-sighted policy. The whole purpose for which we are fighting is the creation of a better world in which the individual will be enabled to develop his own personality.

Our principles and ideals, therefore, must be based on true ethical and scientific foundations. One of our urgent duties is to find out what these foundations are. If our old social and religious brakes have been removed, it does not follow that we are to encourage complete licence—a sort of do as you please attitude. On the contrary, we have to find new standards that will be acceptable to society. The regulation of sexual behaviour is essential if we are to have a cultural civilisation. Dr. Joseph Unwin's book, *Sex and Culture*, shows that where there has been no regulation of sexual behaviour there was little interest in the spiritual aspects of life, no culture and no real civilisation. In the past, this regulation has been based on false premises —taboo and irrational fears, misplaced religious zeal and dogmatism. We have outgrown this era just as former sections of the human race outgrew their more primitive ideas. We have to find a new sexual ethic which will embrace so much that is good that the cultural life of the community will develop out of all bounds. This is possible because of the immense advance that has been made in scientific understanding and psychological knowledge. We must pay more attention to these facts even if we are at war.

Masses of young men and women are in the Services; many more are working long hours in factory and munition works. We have already seen that the majority of men in the Services receive lectures on the subject of venereal disease. They must necessarily pick up much more information. There is little doubt that they could well benefit by some supplementary teaching on the ethical and psychological aspects of sexual behaviour.

Some of the younger generation say that as they are unlikely to outlive the war they may as well make hay whilst the sun shines. But this is very often a mere excuse for behaviour that is by far from being ideal. It is often a cloak for a lax system of social behaviour which is devoid of positive purpose or ideal. This is a fatalistic policy which is fundamentally unsound and selfish. It is by no means certain that we are all going to be killed. Some of us will be, of course, but it is a poor philosophy to go about expecting death at any moment.

Life in the Services should be looked upon as a testing place in which the individual can do everything in his power to prepare for his return to civil life. He can develop his health and physique; find new interests and make new friends, or he can just drift. In one respect army life is unnatural. Vast quantities of men are herded together without sufficient opportunity of meeting girls in a natural manner. This may lead to a coarsening of mind, more especially as many of the women who hang around camps are not a very desirable type. There is no use in minimising the fact that many girls, especially the younger ones, look upon all men in uniform as heroes to whom they must naturally give everything. Having very few principles and little knowledge of life, they are only too eager to be accommodating. If a venereal disease is not caught it by no means follows that a pregnancy is avoided, and many a man finds himself faced with the unpleasant necessity of marrying a woman with whom he is not really in love. Contraceptives are by no means 100 per cent safe when obtained indiscriminately, and even in peace time there are about 25,000 illegitimate births, to say nothing of the high abortion rate. Although a couple may think that sex intercourse is merely a "bit of fun" they forget that once the girl's feelings are aroused she may really fall in love with the man or alternatively she may become very upset and ill if, for any reason, the relationship is brought to an end. In this case she may try one man after another in the hope of satisfying an intolerable urge, and the result is often disaster. The type of relationship we have described on page 88 is often developed under those conditions.

In spite of all the difficulties of the present situation, one cannot help feeling that if a couple fall in love they should marry as soon as possible. None of us know what the future will produce, but it is silly to refuse to face facts— to hold back and remain at the bottom of the ladder. Progress is essential to happiness; marriage is one of the essential steps. Even if the worst should happen, it is very unlikely that the girl will ever regret her decision, especially if it has been possible to obtain the help and advice suggested in the earlier chapters of this book. The war marriages that go wrong are those that would go wrong anyway and are due to other causes than that of war. On the other hand, it must be admitted that these marriages are often carried on under great difficulties; the couple see each other very infrequently and often have no home of their own. Nevertheless, it is a great thing to be married

and to have the opportunity of facing up to these difficulties together. This leads one to say a word about having
children in wartime. It is a fundamental urge in women
to re-create where they see wastage, and as war is necessarily
a wastage of human life, women naturally feel an instinctive desire to have children. They may not be consciously
aware of this feeling but it is there, nevertheless. Here
again even if the worst should happen the girl has her baby
and her memories—not just memories and regrets. This
fact is not sufficiently appreciated by men.

There are one or two other matters which follow
naturally from the foregoing discussion. There is a type of
man, unfortunately fairly commonly found in the Services,
who will tell the younger men that they are not men at all
until they have "had a woman", and proved their
capability as men. They usually add that intercourse is good
for a man and if not practised regularly will make him
impotent; that is to say incapable of performing the sex
act properly, or will produce various other unpleasant
physical conditions. This is all nonsense. There is not a
scrap of evidence to support their arguments, which are
wholly pernicious. Many men go for years without sex
intercourse and yet are perfectly healthy and able to
perform the act should occasion arise. The causes of
impotence are almost always psychological and due to an
entirely different set of circumstances. Indeed, it would
be nearer the truth to say that the sort of intercourse
recommended by these advisers is likely to produce just
that situation they are professing to cure. Many a man
has taken this advice and then, when marriage occurs,
has found himself impotent because of the inhibitions
aroused by feelings of guilt and fear due to the previous
experience. That sort of advice will get us nowhere.

SOME PRACTICAL SUGGESTIONS

Let us consider what can be done both now and when
the war is over. Before the war started, an organisation

known as the Marriage Guidance Council prepared a
syllabus of lectures which could be given to groups of young
adults from 18–25 years old. The lectures, usually three in
number, were designed for mixed audiences. Their purpose
was to give people the information which they should have
had when they were young and to supplement this with
more advanced knowledge useful to them at their present
age. The syllabus of these lectures is given in Appendix A
and indicates the subjects which were considered most
valuable. Many well attended lectures were given by
various lecturers up and down the country. There is no
doubt that they met a real need. They were given in public
halls, chapels and churches.

Going back a little farther in the age groups, we come
to the schools. Much valuable work has been done in
elementary and secondary schools, particularly in South
Wales by two lecturers of the Alliance of Honour—Mr.
Tucker and Miss Pout. They have taught thousands of
children in school groups and have explained their methods
in detail in two books, *Awkward Questions of Childhood* and
Sex Education in Schools. These lectures have necessarily
been confined to children up to about fifteen years of age.
They should be provided in every elementary and secondary
school throughout the country. What about the boy between
15 and 18? In many cases he has already left school and is
working in a factory, mine or office. His only hope of getting
any proper advice lies in chance instruction from some
outside agency such as club, scouts, Y.M.C.A. and so on.
If he is still at a public school, he probably gets some
advice from his masters, but this is haphazard and depends
upon the personal views of the masters. This may take
the form of a "jaw" when he enters or leaves the school,
or some arrangement may exist in the school whereby
each housemaster makes a point of interviewing the boys
in his own house when he thinks fit. In addition, the head-
master may talk to all the leavers at the end of their last
term. Here again, the information given in these talks
varies enormously; some being so inadequate as to be more

or less useless, some being little better than a moral lecture based on fear and a bad religious approach, whilst a few are so excellent that they could not be bettered. In most schools, boys now receive an adequate instruction in biology but even here the physiology and anatomy of human reproduction is often left out, or at best treated very indifferently, whilst the psychological aspects are rarely considered. These methods are haphazard and do not provide a general basis of knowledge or any real continuity of thought. Nor is there any certainty that the help will be given at the right time.

One of the chief objections to the whole system of individual talks is that the boy instinctively feels that sex is treated differently from other subjects; that one can talk about art, music or mathematics but not about sex, at least not in a sensible open-handed way; that one cannot learn about these things in class as is possible with every other subject. It is more than likely that this attitude of mind has already been established before the boy ever gets to the school. Nevertheless, it could easily be corrected at this early stage. Individual discussion is of immense value and indeed essential provided it is set in the right context. In conjunction with a carefully prepared system of lectures it can be of immense value.

Another disadvantage of the system is that it by no means follows that a housemaster, or for that matter a doctor or a parson, is capable of giving this information without adequate training. During the last three or four years the writer has had the opportunity of visiting various public schools every term in order to give a more detailed course of instruction to various age groups, which seems to be of some value. For this purpose the boys are divided into three main groups; the new-comers who are pre-adolescent; the 16 year-old group and the leavers. These three divisions correspond with three definite developmental stages in each of which the boy apparently needs a particular kind of help and information. The new-comers, being pre-adolescent, are largely concerned with facts.

The information given to this group could really be given a few months earlier, whilst they are still at their preparatory schools. Indeed, there is considerable evidence that these schools are not fulfilling their responsibilities in this matter. Not yet being emotionally conscious the boys' interests are mainly concerned with the mechanics of sex, rather than with the emotional side. They want to know how the engine works. It is most important to give this information in the simplest and clearest manner and, in particular, to indicate the difference in the development of the sexes. The emotional differences that will arise in later life are outlined very simply. The best way of giving this information is in collaboration with the biology master. It is not sufficient to deal with sex matters in a biological setting, but the biological approach is the right one. All the groundwork is to be found in biology, the physiological and psychological aspects can be added later. An attempt is being made at one school to give a joint biological and medical talk, which is fitted into the ordinary school syllabus. There are excellent slides and films available which can make such a combination easy and interesting. [1]

The main problem which seems to occupy the boy's mind from about 15–17 is his relationship to and mode of behaviour with his companions. Psychologically speaking he is passing through the homosexual phase, so it is natural that his interest should be directed to this aspect of his life. His emotional relationships with other boys, his physical growth and sexual development, nocturnal emissions and the problems connected with self-stimulation are his main concern. It is with these phases of sex activity, therefore, that the second lecture is designed to deal.

When the boy is leaving school and going out into the world, it is obvious that he requires help and information about the problems that will face him in his new surround-

[1] It is hoped to issue shortly a small book giving details of all three lectures.

ings. He needs to understand the emotional differences between the sexes and the principles upon which sexual behaviour should be based. He wants to know about pre-marital relationships, abortion, contraception, and the factors affecting marriage. Above all he is interested in the underlying psychological principles of sexual behaviour. Whilst factual information necessarily predominates it is set in a background of ethical principles; indeed, the facts are used to illustrate the disorganisation and tension that disturbs the personality if practice and ethics are at cross purposes.

Thus there is much to discuss and it has been found useful to allow time for questions and discussions afterwards. Opportunities are also provided for the boys to discuss their own individual problems in private, a privilege which is usually exercised to the full.

The lectures are designed to show the boys the naturalness of their sex feelings and to encourage them to talk to their housemasters, the school medical officer or their parents, whenever they wish. It is not intended that the lectures should take the place of the help given by the housemaster, but rather strengthen the bond between him and the boy. It is obvious that both methods of approach have their place and each should supplement the other. Ultimately, of course, it should be possible to design courses of lectures on the wider aspects of social psychology in the universities and colleges in which many of these boys will spend the next few years of their lives. This system of instruction could well be extended to other sections of the community. If it is useful in the public schools it is equally valuable for the young factory worker. It should be, and is being, applied to girls as well as boys, the lectures being adjusted to their particular requirements.

The requisite for a new order involves, amongst others, the following points:

1. An acceptance of a positive motive in life based upon a real sense of vocation.

2. A reorganisation of economic and environmental conditions which will enable the ideals we have formulated to have a trial.
3. A constructive and widespread attack on various social ills like abortion, slums, and the infant death rate, so that the family unit can be strengthened and developed.
4. The re-establishment of motherhood as a positive factor in the life of the community.
5. An acceptance of the principles of sex equality, mutual love and the production of healthy children who are wanted, properly spaced and sensibly educated.
6. A recognition of the rightful and positive use of emotion.
7. A refusal to accept false values and outworn dogmas.
8. A widespread educational policy based on a working partnership between science and religion.

We cannot hope to achieve these results unless our teachers are themselves well versed in these principles and realise the necessity for a more positive attitude to these matters. This applies particularly to the clergy, to schoolmasters and to doctors. Of the first two groups we have said enough already. What of the medical profession? It is an unfortunate fact that many doctors are unwilling to give constructive help and in many cases regard educational endeavours of this nature as being outside their terms of reference. Why is this? Two reasons may be considered. In the first place there appears to be a widespread misconception in the minds of many medical men and women of their real purpose in professional life. They are more concerned with the cure of disease than with its prevention. The science of medicine as we know it to-day is comparatively new. Indeed, it is only within the last hundred years or so that the doctor has really had sufficient knowledge and equipment to deal with disease. Antiseptics, anæsthetics, and X-rays are of very recent date, as is our knowledge of physiology and bacteriology. All this new knowledge has had to be assimilated and put in its proper perspective. The profession has been mainly concerned with the new possibilities of cure that have opened up. And rightly so. Nor is the task finished. We have seen how much remains to be done even in the small field we have been discussing. Nevertheless, the past few years have tended to concentrate the thoughts and endeavours of doctors towards the prevention of disease and ill-health. Here again, we are only just beginning to understand the important part that sex and marriage disharmonies play in the health of the individual. Doctors, like lay people, have their ethical background. They too have been disturbed and upset by the general upheaval of thought through which we have been and still are passing. They too have to reconsider their philosophy.

The role of the doctor as educator, therefore, is a new conception to which many are not yet adjusted. But if we are to prevent disease we must be willing to teach people how to live; how to build up healthy bodies and minds. Thus the progressive doctor finds himself spending more and more time in trying to find the source of his patient's trouble, not only by looking down a microscope or removing a diseased organ, but by trying to understand the motives and mechanisms of his patient's life style, and by correcting it when he finds it directed into wrong channels. And so, whether he likes it or not, he must concern himself with education, whether it be directed towards the better education of the young, the necessity for immunisation against diphtheria, or the prevention of marital disharmony. In order to do this effectively he himself must be properly educated. The second reason, therefore, why the doctor often fails to deal with sex matters in a more positive manner is because he never received proper training in these matters whilst he was a student. It is an unfortunate fact that the majority of medical students receive practically no instruction in sexual psychology or for that matter in the principles of contraception. There is only one teaching hospital in London, for instance, which gives adequate contraceptive advice in a clinic. If the students want information they have to find it out for themselves, or attend some clinic on their own initiative, very often after they are qualified. It would be quite easy to attach an efficient clinic to every gynaecological department and equally easy to provide a short annual course of lectures on the principles of sexual psychology in the final year. Such reforms are long overdue and are essential before doctors can be expected to discharge their duties to their patients effectively.

This book must end on a personal note. Some readers may feel that too much emphasis has been placed on religion; that it is useless to attempt to find any common ground with orthodox religion, and that the Church must be replaced by something more live and in harmony with modern thought. They may be right. Others will say that I have gone too far in the other direction; that the troubles of this world and, of course, of our sexual morality, are due to the natural sinfulness of our natures and that there is very little to be done about it until we show a real change of heart. They too may be right, but I cannot agree with either point of view. The one refuses to see anything good in the past; the other fears to look into the future. The one muddles up the teaching of the Church with that of Christ; the other is far too negative and self-centred. Both put emphasis in the wrong direction. Must we not distinguish between Christ's teaching and that given by his followers?

Religion is evolutionary, not static; accepting new facts, moving with the times and adapting itself to an ever-changing society. Much Church teaching and behaviour in the past has been cruel, intolerant and selfish. Have we not outgrown that era? Christ's message, however, is positive, dynamic, unselfish and very simple. It is concerned with personal behaviour and our neighbours' well-being; indeed it demands that one's life should be devoted to helping other people.

There appear to be two main types of religious people. Those that think religion is a personal affair largely concerned with their own spiritual state, and those who think that the way to understand God and obtain spiritual insight is through daily work and public service. We have concentrated too much on the first and not enough on the second. We have concerned ourselves too much with ritual and outward show; in making everyone conform to some particular code of public or personal morality. We have yet to try a Christian religion that is directed towards the well-being of other people—both in public activities and private relationships. That the best minds in the Church are alive to these issues is shown by the report given in *The Times* of January 11th, 1941, on the conclusions of the Malvern Conference. The ultimate ownership of the principal industrial resources of the community by private owners is condemned as being likely to encourage these owners to work for themselves and their own advantage. "As a consequence a way of life founded on the supremacy of the economic motive will remain, which is contrary to God's plan for mankind."

I do not think we will get any positive change in sexual morality until we alter our economic situation, and until we build a society fit for people to maintain their personal ideals.

Most of our religious life is based on snobbery. The quality sit in one part of the church, the labourers in another. We have many false values. Creeds and dogmas, and a particular type of ritual have too much significance for some people. The spiritual life of the community is not dependent upon these things or even upon its churches, although public worship is one of the necessary facets of religious life. If our churches were all bombed we should not lose our spiritual life. Indeed, we might learn to love our neighbours better. To say that religion is dead or unnecessary is to show an ignorance of man's fundamental needs. Man has a spiritual nature. It must be satisfied because spiritual power is necessary to the life of the community. Its force, however, needs new direction. There must be less talk about the benefits of the world

to come and more about the job we have to do in this one.
And finally a sense of spiritual values is necessary if we are
to create the type of citizen who feels he has a contribution
to make in building a new social order based on individual
freedom and the elimination of selfish ends in our public or
private lives.

APPENDIX A

MATERIAL FOR LECTURE COURSES

PREPARED BY THE MARRIAGE GUIDANCE COUNCIL

For the use of the Council's lecturers only.

The amount of material presented, and the method of presentation, will vary according to circumstances and at the discretion of the individual lecturer.

INTRODUCTION

Marriage relationship—unique—permanent.,
Marriage a starting point, not a goal. An art to be studied, the main outlet for sex energy.

It involves the whole of human nature, physical, mental and spiritual.

PHYSICAL ASPECT OF MARRIAGE

1. Physical side often leads to difficulties if imperfectly understood. Therefore brief account of male and female organs, including action of testes and ovaries. Hormone action. Cyclical activity and emotional variations. Menstruation.

2. The value of the physical relationship in marriage is immeasurable to both husband and wife. Therefore it should be wholehearted on both sides; no grudging nor withholding nor fear. Very valuable for the couple to discuss it straightforwardly together beforehand. When

Oa

first intercourse occurs, man must advance slowly because his desire grows more quickly than the woman's. It may take some time to manage it so that both reach the climax at the same moment. Importance of learning art of love. No need to be disappointed if success is not achieved at once. Skill will come with practice and experiment. If difficulties arise, it is wise to seek expert advice.

3. Continence and self-control are often called for by circumstances, and are part of the useful discipline of living in couples. Consideration for each other may require them.

4. Transference of sex energy and how to achieve it. Different problem for married and unmarried. Value of creative work.

5. Great advantage of pre-marital consultation for both man and woman, also medical examination to establish freedom from transmissible defect or disease. Marriage may be right for couples who should not have children. (Advice from a Eugenic expert may be obtained through the Council.) General principles of heredity.

6. Sexual relationship in marriage should bring happiness to both man and woman equally. It should always come as the climax of love-making.

Technique of Coitus[1]

(*a*) Nature of coitus. Three stages. Importance of right approach.

(*b*) Nature and purpose of hymen. Methods of dealing with it.

(*c*) Positions. Name them. Each pair will find what is most satisfactory for themselves.

(*d*) Frequency. Need for satisfactory mutual adjustment.

(*e*) Possible difficulties in coitus: Frigidity. Impotence. Premature ejaculation, etc. These may be set up by:

[1] Only for lectures to those on the eve of marriage.

(i) Physical causes; (ii) Bad technique; (iii) Wrong psychological attitude. Can usually be helped or cured. (Need for positive approach and encouragement.)

7. *Parenthood*

(*a*) To fulfil both a biological urge and a social duty, children are necessary. Refusal of healthy couples to have children a great mistake.

(*b*) Necessary to prepare beforehand for parenthood—home for child, mother able to look after it, etc. Danger of debt.

(*c*) Planned parenthood. Methods of planning the arrival of children:

    (i)   Leave entirely to Nature.
    (ii) Abstention from intercourse.
    (iii) "Safe period."
    (iv) Coitus interruptus.
    (v)   Use of scientific contraceptives.

Pros and cons of all five methods. Dangers of indiscriminate use of advertised contraceptives without medical supervision. Necessity of talking over whole position with an expert.

(*d*) Sterility. Causes. Can often be cured by medical treatment. Both partners need investigation.

(*e*) Abortion (within marriage). (i) Natural—need not be alarming, but must be properly treated by a doctor. (ii) Artificial—unless for medical reasons and carried out by a doctor, this is not only illegal but also dangerous to the mother and ethically wrong.

(*f*) Pregnancy. Importance of consulting a doctor soon after first missed period. Now possible to diagnose pregnancy after a fortnight.. Intercourse during pregnancy usually permissible in modified form. Best avoided during third month and last six weeks. Positive approach to child bearing. Freedom from fear. Influence of mental outlook on physical well-being. Value of breast feeding.

MENTAL AND SPIRITUAL ASPECTS OF MARRIAGE

1. *Right Approach to Marriage*

(*a*) Nature of sex instinct. Sex much bigger than a mere physical relationship.

(*b*) Inadequacy of promiscuous relationships, petting parties, etc. Dangers:

(i) Selfish and superficial relationship, based on ignorance and irresponsibility.

(ii) Possibility of pregnancy, which may lead to unhappy marriage, illegitimacy or abortion.

(iii) Increased likelihood of difficulties in later life.

(iv) Danger of venereal disease.

(*c*) Choice of a mate. Great importance of compatibility, physical, mental and spiritual. Important considerations: Difference of race or religion—clear justification required for disregarding these. Discrepancy of age—age of woman should never be much greater than that of man (important to children).

Hereditary weaknesses should be known to both partners and faced before marriage. Some chronic diseases may only be discovered by pre-marital examination.

(*d*) "Engagement" period. Necessity for each couple to find a method of lovemaking which can be reconciled with their consciences and which leaves them happy and satisfied, not tense and irritable. Decision must be made, and loyally kept, as to how far they can safely go with mutual endearments. Importance of working, playing and talking together. Community of interests. Some standards of values. Not a mere physical attraction. For each the wellbeing of the other person should be the first essential. Objections to sexual relationships during the engagement:

(i) Feelings of fear, guilt and shame may spoil a free and spontaneous relationship and make it appear furtive and sordid.

(ii) Always a possibility that a child may result.

(iii) Great emotional changes, especially in the woman, are set up, which may make it difficult for the partners to make a readjustment to life if the relationship is severed.

(iv) Such an experimental union is nothing like marriage itself, and can provide no criterion.

(v) The physical side is over-emphasised and out of proportion.

(e) Need to encourage earlier marriages. Contentment with simpler standards of living.

2. *Marital Harmony*

(a) Necessity for complete honesty and frankness on all points, including money. Willingness to forgive imperfections.

(b) Living in parents' homes is usually inadvisable. Psychological ties to parents may be obstruction to development of full married love.

(c) Contention in the home is fatal to the best development of the children.

(d) There must be complete equality of status between husband and wife. Realism in attitude to each other. Danger of "ideal pictures" which do not square with the facts. Question of obedience.

(e) Complete abolition of old idea of man's "right of demand" (sexually). Nor must the woman be selfish in her demands.

(f) Sharing of work and interests.

(g) Need for each to have independent friendships—friends of both sexes. Both welcome in the home.

(h) Importance of wife having outside interests. Problem of full or half time work for married women.

3. *Marriage a Creative Union*

(a) Married life the normal life. In it personalities develop to their richest fulfilment.

(*b*) Man, wife and family as social unit—evidence of history. Importance to the individual and to the race of happy, stable home. Relation between broken homes and juvenile delinquency. Need for honesty and frankness in answering children's questions on sex matters.

(*c*) Marriage a developing relationship through the years. Cannot be mastered in months. The inevitable ups and downs of marriage—ultimately become links between husband and wife and lead to greater unity. Difficulties tend to disappear if talked over in full confidence. Need for each partner to respect the personality of the other. (Sum of whole matter.)

(*d*) Need to see home as part of wider world. Not just selfish satisfaction in each other, but together giving something to the life of society.

APPENDIX B

TO THOSE ABOUT TO MARRY

(Pamphlet issued by the British Social Hygiene Council)

This publication includes discussion on certain matters not comprised within the policy of the Council. It does not, therefore, form part of its official publications.

1. In thinking about marriage the important thing is to be sure what marriage really is. Some people are content to think of it as a partnership; and when we are clear that it is a partnership between equals we have learned something essential about marriage. But there is a deeper side to it; and a great deal of the misery in the world comes from people not understanding this. True marriage is not a partnership which can be altered or broken at will, but the development of a new and permanent relationship between two people.

2. Marriage is not the goal but the starting point of a great adventure. It is a union of body, mind, and spirit, and its only true foundation is real love and mutual respect. Love is much more than mere physical attraction. Husband and wife need also to be good friends, sharing the whole of life together, learning to work and play together, as well as to make love. This will create a real sense of comrade- ship, so that when difficulties arise, as of course they will, they can be tackled with understanding and good humour.

3. A woman is right to look for a healthy husband, a man for a healthy wife. It is strongly urged, therefore, that both should see a doctor before marriage:

Firstly, to find out the truth about their general health, because a doctor can often help to improve it.

Secondly, to find out whether they have any weaknesses or inherited diseases, which might be a reason against marriage or against parenthood. It is cruel to pass on any disease to children, and in some circumstances marriage without children may be the right course.

Thirdly, to learn how sexual intercourse can be happily and healthily managed. Its mismanagement is a common cause of unhappiness in marriage.

4. It is also a good thing to see a doctor after marriage if there have been difficulties or disappointments in intercourse. A doctor can frequently explain them and put many things right. Often the mind can be cleared by question and answer when books on the sex side of marriage have failed. Some of them are excellent, but they may not meet the particular point that is giving trouble.

5. It is important to remember in intercourse that the woman needs satisfaction as much as the man. This may not be obtained in the first experiences of married life, but most difficulties can be overcome with patience and perseverance. The idea that self-control is unnecessary in the married state and that a husband has a right to demand sexual relationships whenever he wishes has caused much misery in marriage. Sexual intercourse is only happy and successful when both desire it, and it should be the last act of a process of real love-making. On the other hand, a willingness on the part of each to meet the other halfway is essential.

6. Children are the natural completion of marriage, and the greatest bond between husband and wife. Healthy couples who deliberately refuse to have children are acting both selfishly and unwisely; they are missing one of the greatest joys in marriage. If a couple who desire children have not had any after two years of marriage, they should certainly seek medical advice. It is often possible to set the condition right.

7. It is the right of every child to be desired and prepared

for in advance. No couple should bring into the world children for whom they cannot provide the necessaries of life, though it is important to avoid exaggeration as to what such necessaries are. In any case, for the sake of the wife's health it is important that children should be wisely spaced, and many couples find that for various reasons it is better not to have a child at once, as for instance when they have to live in somebody else's house or when the wife has been working hard right up to the time of marriage.

8. If it is decided to postpone the birth of a child, the couple should seek advice on conception control from a doctor or clinic. It is unwise to employ methods learned from advertisements, as they may not be suited to the particular case and may cause a great deal of harm to either partner or to both, and even to future children. Prolonged abstinence in marriage is undesirable and uncompleted intercourse may have serious consequences. So if children are to be "spaced" it is wise for both husband and wife to consult a doctor.

9. It should be remembered that once a baby has been conceived no pills or drugs should be taken or anything done to bring about a miscarriage, as this is not only illegal but also may cause serious damage to a woman's health.

10. A great many marriages are spoilt by worries and quarrels about money, but this need not happen. If husband and wife are perfectly frank with each other about their earnings, what they spend, and what they can save, then, as they plan to make ends meet they may even be drawn closer to each other. Many husbands, and many wives also, will find that they must give up expensive and unnecessary habits which were formed before marriage. There must be no secrets, no cheating of each other. An agreed sum should be set apart for housekeeping, clothes and essentials and then a certain sum for pocket-money for the husband and for the wife. The burden of debt has spoilt many marriages, and it is extremely important not to start in debt and to avoid it subsequently. Wherever the

income permits it is very desirable to put by a little margin for unforeseen expenses, such as illness or loss of work.

11. Good housekeeping and good cooking help to make happy husbands. If a wife has not had the chance to learn these things before marriage it is very important that she should do so as soon as possible afterwards. It is also a very happy thing for both when husbands are willing to take a share of the housework and the care of children. These are heavier burdens than most husbands know.

12. Marriage is an equal partnership and decisions should be made by both together. Sometimes leadership will come from one side and sometimes from the other.

13. Love is like a fire, and it needs attention if it is to be kept alive. Husbands and wives are apt to "settle down" and leave no time for being nice to each other. They often neglect one another through thoughtlessness. It is very well worth while to take trouble to win fresh love by fresh love-making, and by showing that they still value each other. Many couples find that they are making new discoveries after several years of married life.

14. In all marriages men and women must be willing to accept each other as they are. It is a great misery for a man to picture to himself what his wife should be and then to grow angry because the real wife is not exactly like the picture. The same is true for a wife. We all have faults, and most of us are at times annoying. Many of us have irritating habits which can cause difficulty in marriage, while nagging is a quite fatal enemy to real joy. In fact, there has to be a great deal of give and take throughout the whole of married life.

15. Those who marry must do so with the intention of holding together through the whole of life. Those who are ready to part rather than to try again can never hope for success and happiness in married life. The best period in marriage sometimes comes after the two have had difficulties and even quarrels. If they learn to overcome these things they are well on the road to success.

16. Success in life, in marriage, and in the upbringing of children is gained by patience, unselfishness, good humour, understanding and forgiveness. Marriage is infinitely more than a matter of bodily and mental relationship. Success in it depends ultimately upon spiritual insight and power, and those who have tried this way know how they are helped to face life's problems with confidence and calmness. Many people seem to neglect this side of life altogether, but its rightful development and use will strengthen and deepen the comradeship of husband and wife. It will enable them to bring courage and devotion to their common responsibilities and cares; it will make their home a place of friendliness, refreshment and peace for all who dwell in it and for those who visit it. Spiritual insight and power are found most surely in the knowledge and worship of God and the search for these is enriched and deepened when undertaken by husband and wife together.

For Product Safety Concerns and Information please contact our EU
representative GPSR@taylorandfrancis.com
Taylor & Francis Verlag GmbH, Kaufingerstraße 24, 80331 München, Germany

www.ingramcontent.com/pod-product-compliance
Lightning Source LLC
Chambersburg PA
CBHW062025270326
41929CB00014B/2320

9 7 8 1 0 3 2 7 9 9 9 3 3